GOOD GIRLS
/BAD GIRLS

GOOD GIRLS /BAD GIRLS

Feminists and Sex Trade Workers Face to Face

Edited by
LAURIE BELL

The Seal Press

For all the bad girls working to make it better

Published by arrangement with The Women's Press, Toronto.

Cover design by Laurie Becharas.
First edition, October 1987
10 9 8 7 6 5 4 3 2 1

Library of Congress Cataloging-in-Publication Data

Good girls/bad girls.

Proceedings of a Toronto conference on the politics of prostitution and pornography, held Nov. 22-24, 1985.
1. Prostitution—Canada—Congresses.
2. Pornography—Social aspects—Canada—Congresses.
3. Feminism—Canada—Congresses.   I. Bell, Laurie.
HQ148.G66 1987   306.7'42'0971   87-16713
ISBN 0-931188-57-1

Seal Press
PO Box 13
Seattle, Washington 98111

CONTENTS

About the Ontario Public Interest Research Group
OPIRG — TORONTO

OPIRG — TORONTO is an organization promoting public interest research, especially among graduate students at the University of Toronto. OPIRG sponsors many projects, both written and active, on a variety of environmental, social, and political concerns.

Acknowledgments

To the canadian Organization for the Rights of Prostitutes, for raising the controversy; to the March 8th Coalition and opirg for taking it up; to Paula Rochman, Diane Roberts, and the Conference Organizing Committee, for developing this controversy into a conference; to the speakers and participants, who generated 150 hours of material; to Kelly Rico, who painstakingly tranformed those hours into transcripts; to David Orfald and Stephanie Cairns, who interfaced with an illiterate and sometimes unfriendly user; to Brenda Clarke for being the best through the worst; Anne Healy, Nicki Monahan, Walter Murphy, Pamela Walker, and Bernie Topel, for the unceasing support they give to me; to the women at the Women's Press, especially Rona Moreau, who coaxed the transcripts into manuscript form; and most, to Marlene Kadar, who saw a book and an editor in the distance and brought them both forward — to all of you my deepest thanks.

INTRODUCTION

"YOU'RE ALL A BUNCH of fucking madonnas!" That was how Peggy Miller, founder of the Canadian Organization for the Rights of Prostitutes (CORP), described a group of feminists at a dinner in April 1985. A controversy had arisen during the planning by the March 8th Coalition of the 1985 International Women's Day in Toronto, and the dinner had been arranged to continue this important discussion.

It all began when Miller and Chris Bearchill, another CORP member, attended a coalition meeting in February that year to object to the statement, which was to appear in a forthcoming International Women's Day leaflet, that the porn shops along Toronto's Yonge Street were harmful to women. They argued CORP's position — that this statement did not represent the views of women employed in the sex trade industry. After some discussion the coalition decided to delete the statement before the leaflet went to press, but no one could have predicted the long-term implications of CORP's objection. It generated count-less meetings, several potluck dinners, many disagreements, a conference, and now this book. All of these constitute the beginning of a long-overdue discussion between sex trade workers and feminists in Canada.

During that April dinner the sex trade workers threw out two questions to the coalition: How could feminists and sex trade workers begin to talk with one another? And what would be the response of feminists to two government reports — the Report of the Committee on Sexual Offences Against Children and Youth (Badgley Committee report, 1984) and the Report of the Special Committee on Pornography and Prostitution (Fraser Committee report, 1985)? Thus the idea for the conference, Challenging Our

Images: The Politics of Pornography and Prostitution, was conceived.

The conference was sponsored by the Ontario Public Interest Research Group — Toronto (OPIRG). Conference organizing was directed by OPIRG staff and March 8th Coalition members Paula Rochman and Diane Roberts. They were assisted by a Conference Organizing Committee, which was made up of political activists, some Women and Men of Colour, some lesbians, some gay men, and an academic or two. I served as a member of this committee. The agenda for the conference was quite broad, extending beyond the two questions posed to the coalition to include various cultural, historical, and political perspectives on pornography, prostitution, and the images of women in our society. Some of these perspectives were represented by men active in these areas who were serving on the Conference Organizing Committee as well as presenting workshops and participating in the conference. Some of the sex trade workers heard from in this book were also involved in organizing the conference, either as committee members or as individuals offering suggestions and criticism along the way. Right from the organizing stage the conference was unique because it included the participation of such a variety of points of view: men and women, prostitutes and non-prostitutes, anti-pornography activists and anti-censorship activists. In fact, the ability to bring together such a diverse group may be distinctly Canadian. It seems that in other places the separate camps meet in separate quarters.

The task of organizing the conference brought some feminists and sex trade workers into each other's lives. Differences in organizing styles, priorities, and even schedules were obvious. One woman's working hours were another woman's sleeping hours. But even though our worlds could be like night and day, some of us ventured cautiously into the others' lives. Thus the "image challenging" that the conference meant to facilitate began during the actual organization. Sometimes it grew out of our co-operation with each other; sometimes it was a result of agonizing differences of opinion.

One event demonstrated to me the need for feminists to reconsider the way we relate to women who work in the sex trade industry. The occasion was yet another dinner, a potluck dinner — this time bringing together prostitutes and performers who were preparing pieces for the conference. We had hoped that the performers would benefit from meeting with the prostitutes and hearing some of their opinions and stories.

First, I was struck by how risky it was for the prostitutes to meet with a group of strangers; the threat of being revealed to the police must have loomed large. There was also the fear of being subjected to feminist examination and criticism. But these women arrived — and, to my surprise, with lasagna and cheesecake in hand. My image of a prostitute had not allowed for her to be able to cook. We had assumed our traditional role of "good girls" and prepared too much food.

On the door of the house where the potluck was held is a sign that reads, "Thank you for not smoking." But each and every one of the prostitutes who came was a smoker. Only two of the non-hookers were smokers. As a matter of principle the smoking ban was not lifted for the evening, although a compromise was reached when a back room of the house was designated the smoking room.

After dinner the smokers drifted into the back room for a cigarette, and a good conversation got going. Each time we were about to begin the planned agenda, someone else would go for a smoke, and soon others would follow. As a result most of the conversation that evening took place in the back room between the prostitutes and the smoking performers.

Looking back on that evening, I realize that because of our adherence to the non-smoking rule, the prostitutes were relegated to a back room space, an area to which they were accustomed because of laws and social mores. It also appeared that these women felt most relaxed in a casual, conversational setting, smoking cigarettes and swapping stories.

Sex trade workers are right when they say that feminists have formulated their analyses about pornography and prostitution knowing nothing about the real lives of sex trade workers. We don't know each other. We never talk to one another. We perceive each other's struggles to be different and separate. Sex trade workers, like other women, have been kept silent. In addition, they feel isolated not only from society but also from a women's movement that has, they believe, ignored or dissociated itself from women who work as strippers, hookers, and porn artists. Indeed, they have accused feminists of not wanting to know or support them. Now sex trade workers are asking feminists to re-evaluate this attitude, hoping to prompt some changes in feminist analyses of and strategies regarding pornography and prostitution.

The outcome of that potluck dinner — where sex trade workers and feminists got to the same house but largely not into the same room — suggests that both groups need to decide what conditions are necessary for meaningful dialogue. Feminists may have to relax some rules in order that sex trade workers feel sufficiently at ease to speak up. We may need to question whose turf the discussions take place on and whose rules govern them. We may need to examine the kind of language we all use to make sure that we understand each other. Feminists and sex trade workers can expect things to get hazy. Not only the air but also our own preconceptions about each other can get cloudy. The haze and the smoke may be an inevitable result of images being genuinely challenged.

▲   ▲   ▲

Challenging Our Images: The Politics of Pornography and Prostitution took place in Toronto from November 22nd to

24th, 1985. It attracted over four hundred participants from various constituencies — the legal profession, social services, the labour movement, academia, and politics — in addition to feminists and sex trade workers. The conference consisted of five forums, which offered a range of panelists, over thirty workshops, a performance night, information booths, and an "Images of Women" display.

The conference organizers had two major concerns. First, they wanted to make a sincere effort to reach beyond Toronto. In spite of travel costs panelists and participants came from various parts of Canada. Second, they wanted to examine the issues of pornography and prostitution from a Canadian perspective and primarily within the Canadian context. Thus most of the speakers and resource people were from Canada. Let me briefly sketch this Canadian context.

In Canada pornography and prostitution fall under federal jurisdiction and are therefore national concerns. Bill C-49, the recent law dealing with prostitution, continues to be a critical issue for prostitutes across Canada. Bill C-114, the proposed legislation regarding pornography introduced in June 1986, also affects people in every province.

The Canadian-American border has always featured prominently in the anti-pornography and anti-censorship movements in Canada. Because most pornographic material is imported from the United States, pornography legislation affects customs regulations, and censorship activities include border seizures of prohibited material. However, "pornographic" material seized at the border increasingly includes feminist, gay, and lesbian material as well as mainstream male porn. This trend has helped shape both anti-pornography and anti-censorship organizing efforts in Canada.

As if it were not already obvious that this conference was essential, two events occurred during the week before it began, reminding all of us how urgent the need was. First, a prostitute was murdered in a Jarvis Street hotel in Toronto. Immediately afterward, Bill C-49, a law forbidding persons to communicate for the purpose of exchanging sex for money, passed third reading in the House of Commons. The concerns about women's safety and legislation affecting the sex trade, both of which had been addressed by feminists and sex trade workers but from different points of view, were brought dramatically to public attention. These events vividly illustrated the concerns of the conference presenters and participants.

This book comes out of the vast amount of material presented at the conference. Many different voices were heard that weekend — those of lawyers, politicians, union representatives, church members, social service workers, academics, historians, and artists — but I want you to hear the voices of those least heard in the past: sex trade workers and feminists speaking to one another. Although many topics were addressed at the conference — from the influence of the church on sexuality to gay and lesbian porn — the most significant accomplishment was the discussion between "good girls" and "bad girls" — feminists and sex trade workers. This book reconstructs that discussion.

Sex trade workers, historically the "bad girls," and feminists, usually considered "good girls" by comparison, are the most affected and least-heard people. Lawyers, social service workers, and politicians have more opportunities to speak their minds, and exert greater influence on the institutions that regulate pornography and prostitution in our society than sex trade workers and feminists.

Margo St. James, unabashed bad girl and founder of Call Off Your Old Tired Ethics, (COYOTE), kicked off the conference by speaking about good girls and bad girls. She claims that the sexual and moral labelling of women is the great divide between the two groups. Without a doubt it was the image of good girl/bad girl that was most severely challenged during the conference. Despite many other differences of opinion, all the sex trade workers agreed that while they proudly claimed their bad girl identity, it was precisely because of it that they have been excluded from the feminist identity.

The sex trade workers who speak in this collection argue that to be feminist still requires women to be good girls. Women working in the sex trade are obviously disqualified from membership in this club. They must either reform or forfeit their right to call themselves feminists. Given this choice, sex trade workers have opted not to identify themselves as feminists. They have chosen instead to highlight their bad girl identity — the one they have control over — and their consequent alienation from the feminist community. They maintain that it is the definition of feminism that must change in order to include both good girls and bad girls, not they who must conform to a good-girl image so as to be considered feminist. Sex trade workers claim, in effect, to be feminists in exile; excluded from a rightful place in the feminist movement, they demand to be recognized as members of the women's community. As one prostitute remarked, "Feminism is incomplete without us."

In naming this book *Good Girls/Bad Girls*, it is not my intention to legitimize or perpetuate this division of women. I wish, rather, to honestly acknowledge its existence and put before you the current thinking of the good girls and bad girls heard from here.

Not surprisingly, the concerns of sex trade workers and feminists are largely the same: both address past and current legislation on pornography and prostitution, the state, sex, art, racism, and the influence of the dominant culture on our lives. Perspectives and strategies vary as to how to proceed with the dialogue and organizing around pornography and prostitution. The contradictions and disagreements in these discussions testify to the fact that the opposing camps are not unified camps. There are feminists in favour of censorship and those opposed; feminists who view prostitution as legitimate work and those who do not. There are sex trade activists who regard prostitutes as victims in some ways, those who do not; some who propose militant action for prostitutes' rights, others who do not.

This selection attempts to provide the reader with a fair sampling of the diversity of views expressed at the conference by sex trade workers and feminists. But it does have an obvious bias. Its very existence is an assertion that dialogue between sex trade workers and feminists has finally begun — that it is, in fact, wholly worthwhile and absolutely essential for the future well-being of the women's movement.

The women in this book speak about what it means to be good girls and bad girls. They challenge each other's definitions, question who decides these definitions, and analyze the benefits and drawbacks of each identity. And at the heart of it all, sex trade workers ask feminists, "Are we your sisters?" Underlying much of the discussion is the question, How can we be redeemed in each other's eyes? In other words, what are we asking of each other? Sex trade workers are demanding that their experience of sexuality and work be integrated into the feminist vision. Feminists are asking for a variety of things — from the abolition of prostitution and pornography to ways in which feminists can join in solidarity with sex trade workers.

The public nature of the conference was a disadvantage to many sex trade workers. But many took the risk of attending. Anyone who knows the fear of dark alleys and smoky back rooms can imagine the dread of a hooker entering a large public auditorium. It may be that the first responsibility of feminists and sex trade workers is to help each other feel safe in unfamiliar surroundings, to reassure each other when we are paralyzed by the fear of what lurks in unknown territory.

This book is an effort to make the discussion that took place during the conference available to more people. It attempts to give sex trade workers, feminists, and others a look at the lives and views of women who are concerned about pornography and

prostitution. You will find that the feminist-identified con-
tributors appear first. This is the way discussions about pornography and prostitution have generally taken place: sex trade
workers have usually had to speak up in response to feminists'
views and activities. Both groups were represented on the panels
for the initial forums and throughout the conference. Still, sex
trade workers came prepared to speak to a feminist audience, a
group they have heard a lot from in the past but have never been
able to respond to directly.

There was another major issue that I would like the reader to
know about. Each Thursday night during the summer and fall of
1985, when the Conference Organizing Committee met, we
looked at the developing conference schedule and asked: What's
missing? One thing that was missing was a discussion of racism
and its relationship to pornography and prostitution. The gap
was never sufficiently filled despite efforts during the organizing
process to do so.

The problem was that there were few people who could address
the dual issues of racism and pornography and prostitution. That
is, none of the sex trade workers we were in contact with were
Women of Colour, and none were addressing the specific issue of
Women of Colour in the sex trade. It was also difficult to find
feminist Women of Colour who were examining the issues of
pornography and prostitution as they relate to racism. And there
seemed to be no white feminists who had integrated an anti-racist
perspective into their analyses of pornography and prostitution.
Human resources were scarce, which says something about the
priorities of various communities within the women's movement.

In spite of this gap, important issues were raised (see Parts One and
Two). Lesbians of Colour, Martha O'Campo of the Committee
Against the Marcos Dictatorship, and Marie Arrington of the Association for the Safety of Prostitutes all addressed various aspects of
racism in pornography and prostitution. But as was pointed out
during the course of the conference, it was not enough.

Any explosion over pornography and prostitution could have been expected during the conference. Most public forums on these issues, even when limited to a fairly homogeneous group, usually produce lots of "heat," as Mariana Valverde has called it. Well, the blaze at this conference ignited over an incident of racism.

The Saturday evening featured various pieces performed by Toronto artists, most written by themselves. One was an impromptu story told by a male ex-stripper recalling his first stripping experience. It took place in one of the Maritime provinces, and the audience was made up of Native women who had come together to the bar from the reservation where they lived. He described these women as "big as bears" and said that they had probably "chiselled their teeth" in preparation for the steak dinner served before the show. It was clear from the rest of the piece that this artist believed that as a male he was supposed to be in control, but being in unfamiliar surroundings with the task of taking off his clothes was threatening to him. To make his point, however, he used racist stereotypes, and the audience reacted strongly. An audience discussion had to be held before the rest of the show continued.

This incident demonstrates the way the seemingly disconnected issues of racism and prostitution and pornography are connected not only to each other but also to the many concerns facing the women's movement. It is time for the women's movement to integrate an anti-racist perspective into its analysis, include sex trade workers' rights on its agenda, and deal with the complexities that arise from both. As a beginning I have included in Part Three three statements: one from Lesbians of Colour, one from the participants of the Racism in Pornography workshop, and one from me on behalf of the Conference Organizing Committee. All were delivered at the closing session of the conference.

Many complex issues have been raised in the last two years.

This book is intended to stimulate more thought and more discussion, which may eventually provoke us to take action. When I was young, I was told the Bible story of Jesus eating dinner with prostitutes. He was supposed to be a model for all Christians. But I was also aware that my teachers and priests didn't really mean that we should get together with prostitutes — quite the opposite. I was expected to be a good girl and stay away from bad girls.

Now every woman needs to ask herself who really benefits from the separation of these two groups. It has been suggested that good girls have more dinners with bad girls. Do we really mean it?

PART ONE

FEMINISTS
SPEAK

THE CONTRIBUTIONS TO this section have been made by women who identify themselves as feminists. Mariana Valverde takes a close look at sexual politics and its place in the larger feminist project, and she explores the roots of disagreements between anti-pornography and anti-censorship feminists. Susan G. Cole is particularly concerned about sexual violence, and she examines the abuse and exploitation of women employed in the pornography and prostitution industries. Christine Boyle and Sheila Noonan assess the impact of feminist criticism on the laws governing pornography and prostitution in Canada. Lesbians of Colour discuss racism and pornography, providing this section with an anti-racist perspective. Martha O'Campo describes how pornography and prostitution functioned in the Philippines under the Marcos regime and how closely tied these industries still are to American militarism and the tourist trade.

These women outline the major concerns expressed by feminists about pornography and prostitution — from violence against women through imperialism to social control. Their contributions, and the remarks of conference participants in "From the Floor," reveal the diversity of opinion, analysis, and strategies regarding pornography and prostitution that exist within the Canadian women's movement.

TOO MUCH HEAT, NOT ENOUGH LIGHT

Mariana Valverde

MANY FEMINISTS AND PEOPLE who care about the women's movement have recently become disappointed, and maybe even demoralized, because the current debates within the women's movement on sexual issues have generated a lot of heat and not necessarily very much light. I don't object to the presence of heat. The problem is that there isn't very much light. I want to reflect on why this is the case. I have tried to think about how we have got ourselves into this situation that is, more or less, stalemated and why people feel somewhat demoralized.

My first conclusion is that sometimes we, and I speak primarily of feminists and people who participate in feminist debates, get extremely worked up about tactical disagreements. These are disagreements over which law should be used to control pornography or where we should hold a demonstration. We need to identify tactical disagreements as such and not spend too much energy on them because, after all, next week will pass, and either we will have had the demonstration or we won't have had it, and we'll all still be around.

But there are other disagreements that reveal a more funda-mental conflict of views about what women's liberation is. We need to be aware of the theoretical frameworks, the basic views that underlie our opinions and our tactical strategies. What are the presuppositions behind a particular view? What would be the theoretical and practical consequences of these presuppositions, these basic views, being accepted as feminist truths? And also, we have to think about our own personal frameworks. And that is one of the main problems. Very few people even know what their own basic ideas about sexuality really are.

I would like to offer one sample of this kind of thinking by applying these criteria to one particular disagreement I have had. I disagree strongly with the approach to the censorship of pornography advocated by Andrea Dworkin and Catharine MacKinnon. There were several things I could have done once I realized that I disagreed. I could have put a lot of energy into exploring the differences between the American and Canadian legal systems and whether we could implement this proposal. I could have investigated all the intricacies of human rights law and obscenity provisions.

For me, however, it was more important to figure out why I so strongly disagreed with this proposed legislation. So I read some of what Dworkin and MacKinnon had written, not so much on censorship itself, but on related issues: the state, sexuality, and gender. In doing so, I discovered that I had a very profound disagreement with their underlying views on sexuality and its place in feminism.

In my opinion both Dworkin and MacKinnon, in different ways, rely on certain, what I would call conservative, views about sexuality in their theoretical framework. However, they don't often make these views explicit, nor do they always provide evidence to support them. They're not unique in this. Most people who write on sexual issues, including all the commissioners of the Fraser and Badgley inquiries, very seldom make their own views explicit. And they never ask where their views about sexuality came from. In the sex debates people start by taking their own feelings and opinions about sexuality for granted and proceed to build their politics on this rather shaky foundation.

When we talk about sexuality, we tend to rely uncritically on myths and vague feelings that we have about it. One of the most powerful myths is that sexual passion is a natural and powerful force. It's dark, it's irrational, and it originates in the body or maybe in the unconscious. It's something out of control that is constantly threatening to erupt into rape, violence, or at the very least, personal tragedy. This view is, I believe, put forth by Andrea Dworkin in her fiction. She portrays sexuality as essentially predatory, and that includes the lesbian content in her fiction. Lesbian characters are as predatory as the male characters, though perhaps not as violent.

We really have to examine this myth carefully and see if we are incorporating it into our own discussions. This myth certainly has some resonance in women's experience. However, I believe that the reason we experience sexuality as involving physical danger and moral or ethical danger is because it has become a conduit for social relations of domination, such as sexism and racism. And also, sexuality has become a kind of conduit for a whole series of collective anxieties, fears, and doubts.

I'll give an example of this. Some feminists have become completely disillusioned with what used to be known as the "sexual revolution" in the wake of revelations about the extent of male sexual violence. This disillusionment does not come from any greater knowledge of the physiology of male sexuality or from sexual passion in general. It comes, rather, from the fact that we have become much more aware of the amazing social power that adult heterosexual men have exerted by virtue of their social privilege. What we've done to some extent is concentrate on the sexual expression of the power that adult heterosexual men have in this society. It is shortsighted to concentrate so much on the sexual expression of that power when that power is expressed just as much through exploitation on the job, imperialism, or any other expression of the social relations of domination.

Catharine MacKinnon, who is a key figure in the pornography debate, believes that women's subordination to men originates largely in the sexual arena. She says that "sexual objectification is the primary process in women's oppression." She also says that "sex and gender and sexist sexuality are defined in terms of each other," but "it is sexuality which determines gender, not the other way around." She goes on to say that "rape, incest, sexual harassment, pornography and prostitution are not economic issues, they are abuses of sex." If one is going to believe that, one must provide evidence, which I cannot find. I don't mean to cast aspersions on Catharine MacKinnon particularly, but I could not find the evidence to support her claim.

MacKinnon does a disservice to the women's movement by claiming sexuality as the site of women's oppression. It is not sex as sex, per se, that subordinates women and constructs them as feminine and, therefore, as powerless. Women have already been constructed as feminine and therefore powerless.

We can distinguish how work is currently organized along the lines of class and gender and racial discrimination from, on the other hand, what work might be like under some other social arrangement. We don't say work is oppressive; we say working for a multinational corporation is oppressive. And yet when it comes to sexuality, we seem to lose our historical and sociological faculties altogether. We forget that sex, in a traditional hetero-sexual marriage, or some other unequal situation, is not necessarily the same as sexuality in general.

MacKinnon participates in two levels of oversimplification or reduction. First of all, she reduces women's oppression to sexual objectification and sexual oppression generally. Then she speaks about sexuality as though it were something that only men do to women, as though it were a uniformly negative and wholly dangerous area for women. I don't know whether she thinks this or not, but in her discussions she concentrates only on sexuality *qua* dangerous. These are the moves that she has made in the construction of her theoretical framework.

There is no single thing that you can look to as the sole cause of women's oppression. The family, the school system, the media, the workplace, sexual relations, the operation of state agencies, the churches, the administration of health care, the legal system — are all involved in the formation of certain groups as oppressed and other groups as privileged. We can never reduce oppression to one cause. If we were able to do that, our task would be much easier.

Claiming sexuality as the site of the oppression of women tends to reduce the complex social and economic factors that determine our oppression to a kind of quasi-natural phenomenon where sexuality, particularly male sexuality, is static, not something that changes through history. We don't hear from MacKinnon and Dworkin about how men get masculinized or how it might be possible to change the social situation so that male sexuality is no longer channelled into aggressiveness. What is perhaps most important, if we concentrate exclusively on the way in which gender oppression is generated in the sexual arena, we will lose sight of other possibilities inherent in sexuality.

Sexuality can, indeed, be a site of oppression, but it can also be a terrain for the development of women's positive and liberating desires, feelings, and ideas. This is not easy, but it is possible, and if we lose sight of the potential for liberation that is present in our sexuality, we are giving up a whole aspect of women's liberation.

Imagining our desire is as much a part of women's liberation as trying to remove the very real obstacles that now prevent us from realizing our desire. I believe we can generate some light for feminism out of the current debates by thinking hard about the various views of sexuality that underlie conflicting tactical proposals regarding pornography and prostitution. Once we have clarified our frameworks, we can take the opportunity to think about the sexual agenda of the women's movement. We might decide to make the struggle for negative freedom, that is, freedom from male abuse, a priority, but surely we have to keep the positive freedoms in mind as well. If we think only about the negative aspects of sexual freedom, if we see sexuality only as a site of oppression, then we will have a distorted view of sexuality and of its place in the feminist project.

Sexual liberation is definitely one of our more long-term goals. I would be the last person to suggest that we can have sexual freedom here and now if we only shed our inhibitions and mentally pull ourselves up by our bootstraps. I am not a Utopian, contrary to some people's belief. However, I do think that the neglect of our long-term goals can distort our immediate issues and our current practice, as I've attempted to demonstrate in the case of MacKinnon and her view of sexuality.

I believe that the utopianism of a certain brand of feminist sexual libertarianism is a bit naive and out of touch with the reality of most women's lives. But the sexual pessimism of Dworkin and MacKinnon is also out of touch with women's reality, a reality in which sex is neither good nor bad in general but is rather a terrain of contradictions and ambiguity. Sex is simultaneously potentially liberating and potentially oppressive, and that contradictory character of sexuality cannot be glossed over if our feminist project is going to be solidly grounded.

This might seem like a very inconclusive conclusion, but no one ever said talking about sex was easy.

SEXUAL POLITICS: CONTRADICTIONS AND EXPLOSIONS

Susan G. Cole

REPORTS IN THE ALTERNATIVE PRESS about my contribution to a recent conference on sexuality referred to me as "well mannered and non controversial" and "personable." All of these I read to be euphemisms for "boring." Recently an organizer of this conference said, "Please, Susan, when you participate in this panel, do not be confrontational." I said, "So you want me to be boring too." We seem to get it both ways: we're criticized for being too polite, and then we're criticized for being too heated. I think the conference organizer was hoping I would talk about why some of these issues are explosive without making them so. I'm going to try, but I'm not going to promise anything.

I want to talk a little bit about how upset people get about our own personal contradictions. I'm a radical feminist and an antipornography activist and a fan of a pop star called Madonna. This makes people very crazy. I am also a feminist who was extremely depressed over the Toronto Blue Jays' failure to make it to the World Series. This also makes people crazy. It is really important for us to discover our own contradictions and acknowledge how complex our emotional responses are. This is difficult to do when people are so anxious to have everyone fall conveniently into camps.

For example, I do not think state censorship is the worst thing in the world. Now wait! I think that systematic abuse of women by the power of people, usually men, is crucial and important to women's experience and to a feminist analysis. Given that, using state censorship to address this abuse is not the worst thing in the world. This does not mean that I am in favour of it. Similarly, those people whose priority is to fight courageously against state censorship have women say to them, "You don't care about rape and sexual abuse." They *do* care! Things are not that simple.

But even though things are complex, I think we can find some common ground in some issues in the censorship arena. For example, I think the Theatres Act of Ontario is a bad law and we should oppose it. This doesn't mean that there might not be a law written that isn't a bad law. Words like *censorship* are very battered. In Ontario we understand state censorship in the form of the Theatres Act, but I don't think the Minneapolis Ordinance is censorship. Sometimes I get the feeling that the term is so broad and so widely used that if I came up to somebody and said, "I don't like your sweater," they would say, "Hey, hey! Stop censoring my sweater!" This abuses and trivializes the serious issue of censorship.

Some of us are trying to talk about how the sexual system works, the way in which sex is constructed to keep us in our places: men on the top and women on the bottom, both socially and sexually. We speak about sexual constructions like forced heterosexuality; the fact that the social meaning of *male* is fused with sexual dominance and the social meaning of *female* is fused with submission; and the fact that some people think that if there is no violence in a sexual encounter, then it can't really be sex. Whenever we talk about how this sex system works, people think that we have an agenda that's going to be backed up by the state. This is not the case. Within the context of feminism I should be able to describe how I think sex works without people worrying that I have cops coming around the corner.

Because sex is the kind of thing that everybody has or wishes they had, when I start talking about the way in which sex is sometimes used against all of us, people think I'm attacking them personally because, of course, they have sex. For example, some of us have been trying to analyze the way S/M fits into the sexual system. When I do this, people think I'm telling them to stop engaging in these practices. I don't want to tell anybody to stop doing anything. I just want people to understand how all of this works in their lives. If a good socialist told you we eat too much white sugar and meat, thereby supporting certain capitalist interests, you would not think she was telling you not to eat at all.

I am concerned about another problem that has become very difficult for feminists to resolve: How can we describe prostitution as an institution of male supremacy and not put individual sex workers at risk in the here and now? This is a dilemma I hope people will do everything they can to resolve. It's the heavy-duty one for us. When I speak of prostitution as an institution of male supremacy, I refer to it in the same way as I think slavery was an institution of white supremacy. Earlier, in a discussion about cultural contexts, Margo St. James said, "Hey, we didn't ask the slave to reform." My response to that was, "No! We wanted to abolish slavery." How we can do that with prostitution without putting women at risk is, to me, a very serious problem, and it's one that I hope we can deal with.

One last point. As a woman and as a radical feminist, I'm very interested in addressing the fact that there are lots of women who are getting hurt. This isn't a very popular thing to say, but it is still true. The kinds of harms women experience are absolutely systematic. According to the depressing statistics, the percentage of women who will not in their lifetimes experience sexual abuse is 7.8 percent. We cannot deny that women are getting hurt.

I understand where all the denial comes from. First of all, nobody wants to be a victim. And nobody likes to admit they are a victim. I also understand that people don't want to talk a lot about how and why women get hurt because they want to get on with their own work. Sex trade workers want to get on with their own survival and the establishment of their personal integrity. I'm referring to those engaged in prostitution and to some artists who are interested in erotica and who want to express their vision through sexual images of social change. I hope that they succeed, and I hope that we can create an atmosphere in which women who are in the sex industry and who can't escape from it can still work with a minimum of risk.

But I want to make something really clear. As everybody is getting on with their work, some of us are still going to be aware that women are getting hurt. And if women are getting hurt as this work is going on or because this work is going on, I, and I hope other feminists, will be there to do something about it.

GENDER NEUTRALITY, PROSTITUTION AND PORNOGRAPHY

Christine Boyle and Sheila Noonan

This presentation was completed before Bill C-114 (containing the pornography amendments) was introduced to the House of Commons during the first session of the 33rd Parliament. A later version appeared in the Dalhousie Law Journal, *Volume 10, Number 2, in October 1986.*

INTRODUCTION
by
CHRISTINE BOYLE

THE ISSUES OF PORNOGRAPHY and prostitution raise questions about the meaning of equality. They provide examples of inequality in Canadian life and make us reflect on just what our aspirations are for achieving equality. Sheila Noonan and I will be talking about the limitations of gender neutrality as a form of equality. That is, we question whether identical treatment of men and women is the best form that the concept of equality takes with respect to the issues of prostitution and pornography. Identical treatment is sometimes important, but not always sufficient, to create equality. First, I will be describing the move toward gender neutrality in the law on prostitution. Second,

Sheila Noonan will discuss the possibility of a move away from gender neutrality in the law on pornography.

GENDER NEUTRALITY AND PROSTITUTION
by
CHRISTINE BOYLE

Until fairly recently criminal legislation reflected different images of men and women in the parliamentary imagination. The picture was to a certain extent one of separate spheres of deviance. These separate spheres can be summarized quite briefly, if somewhat crudely, as follows:

1. Prostitutes were women and deviant.
2. If not, they were women in need of protection through various procuring offences in Section 195 of the Criminal Code.
3. Males were consumers of prostitution and non-deviant.
4. Or they were exploiters of women.
5. There was an area of overlap in that women as well as men could be guilty of keeping a common bawdy house, and there were no distinctively male or female ways of being disorderly or publicly immoral.

In recent years, however, there has been a marked trend toward making prostitution gender-neutral. In 1972 the woman-specific vagrancy offence was removed. This was the offence of being a common prostitute in a public place and unable to give a good account of oneself. It was replaced by the apparently neutral offence of soliciting — Section 195.1. In the early eighties three changes were made:

1. The procuring offences were made gender-neutral.
2. The presumption that a man living with a prostitute was living on the avails of prostitution was made gender-neutral.
3. A definition of prostitution was added to the Criminal Code, making it clear that a prostitute could be a person of either sex.

This trend continues. Bill C-49, the recent federal legislation that prohibits communicating for the purpose of prostitution, makes it explicit that both prostitutes and customers may engage in criminal behaviour. So there are no longer any separate spheres of deviance on the surface of the Criminal Code. And it seems safe to conclude at this stage that this is settled government policy.

The picture is not quite so clear with respect to judicial decisions. Judicial language suggests that prostitutes are understood to be women, while customers and pimps are understood to be men. Judges appear to think that the difference between men and women is a natural one and therefore properly embodied in the law. Thus challenges to the old legislation under the Bill of Rights equality provision have been unsuccessful.

A recent decision by the Manitoba Court of Appeal makes a "natural difference" approach quite explicit. Chief Justice Monnin said, in a case involving a challenge to the offence of having intercourse with a foster daughter:

> What counsel seems to have entirely forgotten is that the distinction or the inequality or the discrimination as he may call it, does not arise from an Act of Parliament, but from an act of Mother Nature. In that respect Parliament cannot be taxed with an unfair, unequal act, since the sexes by nature are different. Counsel, in his vain attempt to force equality, has mixed apples and oranges and cannot be successful.

This, in fact, is a very sophisticated equality analysis compared to some. In *R. v. Beaulne, Ex parte Latreille* the Ontario High Court rejected the argument that women were discriminated against under the vagrancy offence, an offence for which only women could be punished. The judge said, "It is not all females being found in a public place who must give a good account of themselves, but only females falling within the class of prostitutes and nightwalkers." The language is significant. While the term *nightwalker* seems mainly an archaic term for *prostitute*, it made explicit that a woman walking at night was suspicious and could be required by the police to explain herself.

Some judges resisted the legislative attempt to introduce the gender-neutral soliciting offence. Men would be punished for being pimps and procurers, not prostitutes or customers. In *R. v. Patterson* (1972) a judge decided that "every person" in the soliciting offence referred to women only — an interesting decision that men are not persons. In *R. v. Dudak* (1978), a county court in British Columbia held that customers could not be guilty of soliciting for the purpose of prostitution. Nonetheless, even the judiciary cannot resist the move toward gender neutrality, and there are now hints that prostitutes can belong to either sex.

There is little data to go on with respect to enforcement. It is impossible to tell from crime statistics whether there are different perspectives on male and female roles in the context of prostitution. My impression is that there is no established policy of prosecuting customers. The Nova Scotia case of *Attorney General v. Beaver* (1985) reveals something about enforcement strategies. It was a nuisance case, but it was the equivalent of a British Columbia case where an injunction was sought against prostitutes. While it is clear that people of both sexes contributed to the nuisance alleged in the case, the proceedings were taken against women only, notice being given by posting the names of these women on lampposts in the city.

I believe moves toward gender neutrality are sometimes insignificant, sometimes positive to women, and sometimes negative. I get a better sense of the issue by asking the following question. Let's assume that we had neutral laws, even-handedly enforced against both sexes. Would we feel that we had achieved equality in the context of prostitution?

In a sense that is a ridiculous question because we are nowhere near having equal laws equally enforced. However, at the moment we have to ask ourselves whether gender neutrality in law and in enforcement is a dubious goal within the context of the subordination of women. If we aim at gender neutrality in the law, we are aiming at a symmetrical law. But the context makes the issue asymmetrical in various ways; there are distortions of gender, sexuality, and class.

So what should we aspire to? I think that feminist analysis can give us some helpful insights into our aspirations with respect to prostitution. First, feminist analysis brings to the foreground the differing economic contexts of women as well as the inadequate legal initiatives available to respond to women's poverty.

Second, I wonder if the very construct of prostitution is discriminatory in itself. Women, of course, have little control over the legal and social meanings of prostitution. It is significant that feminist analysis helps us to refuse to isolate the prostitute. If one sees prostitution as a form of sexual exploitation, it is certainly not a unique form.

Last, the law in its present formulation maintains the public-private division rejected by feminists. The law focuses on the public manifestations of prostitution while leaving private sexual transactions untouched. This very contrast should lead us to question the real interests that are being protected by the law. It may form part of the overall structure of state regulation, in which sexual inequality is so pervasive, it is practically invisible.

If one sees inequality in the law as the legal expression of the subordination of women, formal equality or gender neutrality obscures rather than eradicates that subordination. The feminist concern is with the subordination of women in general, subordination that takes somewhat different forms in different contexts, but that, overall, reveals that women have more in common than not. This is why I think concern about prostitutes is not a paternalistic concern, but a natural concern of women about the specific circumstances in which other women find themselves.

The bottom-line question about equality is whether the prostitution of women is part of the overall subordination of women or not. If it is, the punishment of prostitutes, under either gender-neutral or gender-specific laws, compounds that oppression.

GENDER NEUTRALITY AND PORNOGRAPHY
by
SHEILA NOONAN

The feminist critique of pornography has been invaluable in acquainting us with the prevalent images of our sexuality. Pornography presents images of female sexuality that are structured to reflect and restrict the way men and women perceive their sexuality. We have become sensitized to pornography's misogynist messages, to the manner in which it objectifies, degrades, and dehumanizes its participants. We recognize the role such images play in sanctioning and perpetuating male violence against women.

We must address not only the way in which pornography constructs women's sexuality but also how it operates to relegate women to subordinate positions in the social, political, and economic order. What role does the law play in translating the ideology of pornography into the actual conditions of women's reality? Pornography poses a threat to the achievement of meaningful sexual equality. How might we best offset its discriminatory effects?

I want to outline the existing legislation and how it has been traditionally interpreted and raise the question: What vision of the world might substantive equality principles produce when applied to pornography?

Pornography is a contentious issue, and we must begin to explore how an adequate balance between sexual freedom and social control may be struck. The existing obscenity provisions in the Criminal Code make no distinctions on the basis of sex. The Criminal Code neutrally deems obscene "any publication the dominant characteristic of which is the undue exploitation of sex or of sex plus crime, horror, cruelty or violence." For material to be within the ambit of the legislation, sexual exploitation must be a dominant characteristic of the work, and such exploitation must be undue. The latter requirement of "undueness" has given rise to the so-called Community Standards of Tolerance Test, under which the court is required to assess whether a publication has exceeded the accepted level of tolerance in the contemporary Canadian community.

Reading the legislation discloses no story of women's sexuality. It does, however, have a tale to tell us about sex. The obscenity provisions appear in the Criminal Code under the heading "Offences Tending to Corrupt Morals." Judicial history clearly reveals that the law was designed to protect public morality by enforcing basic standards of decency. It seeks to suppress public expressions of sexuality in the name of preserving the moral fabric of the community. Sex in this context is associated with sin. The obscenity provisions, at least historically, were less likely to countenance sexual depictions that did not take place in the sanctioned context of heterosexual marital sex. The law suggests that sexual desire is evil.

The feminist critique, however, is levelled not against the evil of sexual desire per se, but rather against the way in which sexuality is constructed because it is harmful to women. The law obscures the fact that sex is gendered. Hence with increased public acceptance of sexual representations, the community standards of tolerance are applied in a liberal fashion so as to license the proliferation of pornographic material. Civil libertarians can proclaim that the law is progressively permitting freedom of sexual expression. The law, in its moralistic, objective fashion, is blind to the recognition that pornographic depictions serve to legitimize and ensure women's sexual and social oppression. In short, the law is blind to the politics of pornography.

There is, however, recent evidence of a judicial awareness of the limitations of a sex-blind approach to this area and an appreciation of the merits of a gender-sensitive manner of approaching obscenity cases. For example, in *R. v. Wagner* (1985) Mr. Justice Shannon, of the Alberta Court of Queen's Bench, noted that there can be undue sexual exploitation where the participants are portrayed in a degrading or dehumanizing fashion. In *R. v. Red Hot Video* (1985) Chief Justice Nemetz, of the British Columbia Court of Appeal, noted that the degrading vilification of women is unacceptable by any reasonable Canadian community standard. Mr. Justice Anderson, in the same decision, was also attentive to the fact that pornographic images exalt the concept that, in some perverted way, domination of women by men is accepted in our society. Moreover, he noted, "If true equality between male and female persons is to be achieved, it would be quite wrong to ignore the threat to equality resulting from the exposure to male audiences of such violent and degrading material, given that it has a tendency to make men more tolerant of violence to women and creates a social climate encouraging men to act in a callous and discriminatory way towards women."

This judicial trend is significant because it adopts the feminist discourse of degradation, dehumanization, and objectification.

Moreover, a feminist methodology is approached in that sexual representations are contextualized. Such a shift, I would argue, more clearly aligns the existing obscenity provisions with the feminist definition of pornography and is arguably responsive to the nature of the harm threatened by pornographic depictions.

Finally, it acknowledges the threat to women's equality that pornography poses. The law, under the guise of sex-blindedness, legitimizes the status quo and obstructs the achievement of sexual equality. By failing to recognize the implications of pornography's message and to grapple with it, the law both reinforces and facilitates women's subordination. Neutrality and morality, objectivity, and good and evil have become the legal tools by which our reality is masked.

What strategy ought we to adopt to combat the inequality that pornographic images perpetuate? In short, how do we wish to strike a balance between sexual freedom and social control? These questions are pressing ones, for our voice is beginning to be heard. A feminist analysis has created an impact in both the areas of adjudication and proposals for legislative reform — witness the recent Fraser Committee report.

The following discussion, rather than purporting to endorse either position, seeks to explore the relative strengths and limitations of two competing paradigms — namely, sexual freedom and social control — and to see how they would assist us in our pursuit of substantive sexual equality. I would point out here that I don't view these two models as mutually exclusive, nor do I suggest that they reveal the only views of what sexual equality might look like.

Embracing sexual freedom, by adopting a position in which we seek minimal state regulation of sexual depictions, would allow us the greatest potential to develop and explore a feminist erotica or alternative images of women and our sexuality. By not invoking the law's protection, there is less danger of the law being used against us to suppress our views or prohibit presentations of female sexuality that threaten the existing sexual order, such as lesbian sexual depictions. I would also argue that affirming sexual freedom allows clarity of political position. Unlike the New Right, we are not against expressions of sexuality per se. The feminist movement, in taking an anti-pornography stance, has often found itself aligned with members of the Moral Majority or other groups who seek to privatize sex. We must be vigilant in ensuring that sex is not simply relegated to the private realm where women's oppression has long taken place in silence and isolation. The feminist attack on pornography is but part of a larger political campaign against current constructions of sexuality and the implications those constructions have had for women's subordination.

But we must ask: Would the development of a feminist erotica, in and of itself, be sufficient to achieve equality in the social conditions of men and women? Arguably not. Merely producing our own sexual images, which challenge those presented to us by pornography, would not alter the subordinate position of women in society. To assume that it might, places incredible faith in the liberal theory of the marketplace — the notion that truth, good, and justice will ultimately prevail if only we can permit people to see it. As a political strategy for the achievement of equality, it seems at best naive.

We cannot afford to ignore the lessons of history, a history that tells us that sexual freedom, in reality, turns out to be freedom for men to exploit women. We should ask ourselves Catharine MacKinnon's question: Given the present circumstances of gender inequality, what is eroticism as distinct from the subordination of women? Has eroticism become inextricably fused with dominance and submission, with expressions of power and powerlessness, so that representations of heterosexual intercourse are, by definition, depictions of non-consensual sex?

If, on the other hand, we decide to elect social control as our strategy, we may gain protection from images of ourselves that are destructive. However, in seeking the intervention of the state, we must ensure that the rules formulated on our behalf will efficaciously redress pornography's discriminatory effects. Rules can only do so, in my view, if they are tailored to reflect the recognition that pornography is about the promotion of women's oppression. This requires that laws are sensitive to the construction of gender that pornographic images seek to produce. We require laws that deal with pornography rather than obscenity; gender-neutral principles will not achieve this goal. The disparate position of women must be taken into account.

Beyond that we have to strategize about what form of legal redress will best empower women. While it effectively curtails the production and distribution of pornographic material, is the civil law or some combination thereof the best vehicle for promoting legal change? Finally, we must embrace social control cautiously, given that the legal system has often participated in women's subordination and given that laws are still applied largely by men.

In my view the risk that laws will serve only to further the needs of the patriarchy and that the rules will embody male values and male experience can best be offset by an attempt to formulate rules that adopt both a feminist discourse and a feminist methodology. However, even if this were to be achieved by legislation, there is no guarantee that the law, in its application, will not be twisted and used against us.

A new world, free from sexual inequality, would require both sexual freedom and social control. We have a unique opportunity to take a step toward this vision — to discover alternative forms of sexual representations and to develop a strategy for legal reform.

FROM THE FLOOR

PARTICIPANT 1: HI. MY NAME is Peggy Miller, and I am the founder of the Canadian Organization for the Rights of Prostitutes. First of all, I want to say that I'm really pleased with this conference because I'm hearing a totally different tone coming from feminists. In the past feminists have had their kingpins telling them what's politically correct to believe, and they all followed because they weren't sure what the issues were. Today I'm seeing feminists get up and challenge their kingpins and say, "Hey, I can think for myself, thank you. I don't like that." And I really love that move.

Susan Cole, we get down to the point "But it's different when it comes to sex." I ask you, "Well, why is it different?" You believe only in "Let's find a way for prostitutes to escape." Mariana Valverde, you respect our need to work, but as far as giving dignity to the kind of work, you refuse to do that.

What is so terrible about fucking for a living? I like it, I can live out my fantasies. It's being said that there's something sick if you enjoy this profession.

Although this conference is called Challenging Our Images, there's one thing you're not challenging in yourselves still. I want to see this challenged: "Who am I, and what am I to you?" And I represent many other whores out there. There are lots of whores out there who, despite the terrible legal and social environment, enjoy our work. Who am I to you if I enjoy my job? Are we without dignity? Have we got a problem? Are we sick? Let's decide that here.

SUSAN G. COLE: I believe women when they speak, so I believe you when you speak about your own experience. When you say that you like it, I believe you. I want to make sure that it's clear that not all women *do* like it. The fact that they don't means that we should recognize how many women are hurt and are there out of no choice and are there out of coercion, and they're being pushed around.

I *do* think that sex is different. I do think there's a difference between advertising and pornography. I do think there's a difference between bridal campaigns and pornography, although I think both of them are subordinating and advertising for inequality. What I'm interested in is how these institutions, pornography and prostitution, make inequality sexual, make it happen in the sexual arena. That's why I make those distinctions. I'm not saying I love bridal showers.

MARIANA VALVERDE: But they're about sex, right?

SUSAN G. COLE: No. They're about institutions of marriage, and they're about the church. That's what I find offensive about them. I think an advertisement is different from pornography. An advertisement is sexual stereotyping, and that's bad for women. Pornography, I think, makes the inequality, as I said, sexual.

PARTICIPANT 2: My first point is to Peggy Miller. I was a prostitute for eight years, from the time I was fifteen up until I was to twenty-three, and I don't know how you can possibly say, as busy as you are as a lady of the evening, that you like every sexual act, that you work out your fantasies! Come on, get serious! How can you work out your fantasies with a trick that you're putting on an act for? I am here to see what can I do to help, as a woman who survived, who didn't become a junkie, who wasn't murdered like this poor girl the other day. What can I do to help the children, first of all, who are scuffin' in the dust?

Do you know what it's like when you have nothing to eat so you have to go turn a trick to feed yourself at fifteen? Have you ever known what it's like to be without a roof over your head, and you have to pretend to some dude that you like him for the night? Can you count how many tricks you have had? You mean you have that many fantasies? Isn't it about having money to survive? That's all I wanted to do — survive! Some of us are lucky enough to have a job that we like, but most of us just want a job to survive. Right? Can't we teach the women some skills so they can survive? I know that that's your opinion, you like it, but prostitution to me was degrading. I grew to hate it. If I had had to fuck one more of them — boy, I would have killed him!

PARTICIPANT 1: I just can't resist that. I have to come back and answer that. First of all, I want to say I think it's great you came forward like you did. Where the hell have you been, girl? Maybe you'll start contacting the rest of us.

I wasn't saying I enjoyed every experience. When you're doing a fucking car date, and you're in and out of there and it's dirty, that guy is a gungebag. I know that. But I'm talking about when you take prostitution out of that environment — when you've got a guy that sees you as a human being, when he is able to be responsive and not see you that way, when you've got a setting around you that makes you feel dignified instead of on the run. I've seen what prostitution, as a trade, can be like at its best. And it's not nearly what we have now. We have been taught — and when we're going through rehabilitation it's even reinforced —

that we're supposed to feel that we don't have dignity when we're doing that. If any prostitute is in this room and feels that she has no dignity when she's doing that, we want to talk to you.

PARTICIPANT 3: Why is it always the other women's fault? How come whatever it is that's making sex workers feel bad about the way people think about their work is the fault of other feminists, who are concerned about the conditions that other women experience? Why does it detract from the well-being of prostitutes to try to do something about women who are injured by some aspects of patriarchal sexual relations? Why is it feminists' fault?

SUSAN G. COLE: I'm so glad you're here. The reason it's women's fault is because it's always easier to point at women and blame women instead of looking at either the institutions themselves or the men who continue to be privileged by having access to female sexuality through those institutions. It was Flo Kennedy who coined the phrase *horizontal hostility*, and you're looking at it. Another reason is that pornography tells us a lot about who's to blame for everything, and that's women. Women are always to blame for sex. And prostitutes, in particular, are depicted as sexual addicts who are in it expressly for the sex. So the institution of pornography feeds those views of women and what we're for, and what we like, and how we like to get it, and how it feels when we get it, and the way they think we like to get it. And women say it's feminists who are turning us into victims. You'd think that feminism and feminists had invented sexual abuse just to prove the point that male supremacy is bad. We didn't, and I think that a lot of this finger-pointing is a really good illustration of how hard it is to really look at what's going on. Who's benefiting from it? Who gets something out of prostitution? Who gets something out of the fact that there is a population of women who are going to be sexually servicing men for money? It's pretty simple.

PARTICIPANT 4: I would like to know why it has to be the whores, the women and the men in the sex trade, that start saying, "What the hell are you people doing here? Why aren't you listening? What is this good girl/bad girl?"

Sheila Noonan and Christine Boyle are saying things that are really offensive to me because I believe in sexual freedom, and I have a problem with social control without a serious analysis. What is a feminist? What is pornography? We need to analyze "Who are the good girls?" Am I a good girl? Is she a bad girl?

There's a propensity in conferences, where there are so-called experts, to accept what they say as the truth. It may not necessarily be that way. What is, after all, your definition of pornography?

SHEILA NOONAN: First of all, let me start by responding to the last question that was put. I have not purported to give a definition of pornography precisely because I think that it's an important undertaking for all of us, as women, to decide, particularly as we want it applied in a legal context. I hope that I wasn't understood to say that I want social control and not sexual freedom. I think I said quite the opposite: that for me it requires some elements of social control, but that it's really important for women to try to develop our own alternative constructions of sexuality.

Last, I certainly do not hold myself out as an expert. I hold myself out as someone who is here to help participate in coming to terms with these issues. And I said right up front that these are contentious issues. But I don't put my viewpoint forward as *the* only viewpoint, the definitive answer in pornography, at all. I'm hoping that we, collectively, can undertake to define what pornography is and what we want to do about it.

PARTICIPANT 5: I do a lot of child care work. I've worked with a lot of street kids, and I've never yet met a kid who wanted to grow up to be a prostitute. Nor have I ever necessarily met a prostitute, though I've seen people in the business of prostitution. Prostitution is a label that we put on people and one of the hardest labels that those people have to drop when they decide to get out, if they are lucky enough to get out. I think we need to have opportunities for those who want to get out: resources, affordable housing, career options, psychological assessments and treatments, addiction counselling — all those options. What do you do for a girl who gets a three- or four-year fine for one soliciting act and from that point on, if she decides she wants to get out tomorrow, can't be bonded, can't handle money, won't be allowed to work with kids?

There are kids out there who are thirteen, and they can't sign a lease for an apartment and they can't get a job because they're not sixteen, and they can't stay at home because they're being physically abused or sexually abused. We have to look at those issues too. Not all men are into putting women down. I hope we women take our power into our own hands as opposed to pointing fingers. Women also have to look at themselves and ask, when they wear clothes a certain way and take on certain jobs and certain things, what are they getting out of it? When we wear certain kinds of clothing and we buy makeup, are we doing it to please ourselves, or are we sometimes doing it to buy into something? I think some of the responsibility is on us.

PARTICIPANT 6: I don't know where to begin. Number one, about the kids on the street and not having any place to go — that is very true, they don't. In British Columbia they have cut back on the social service programs and safe houses for kids in the street because the Ministry of Human Resources has made the statement that the street kids are not in crisis because they are used to it. I would like to cite the fact that about 90 percent of the kids on the street are also wards of the government. So we think the premier should be charged with gross neglect and being a bad parent.

Number two, I want to challenge you on this thing about what we wear and how we're dressed, and that we're asking for it and we'd better look at why we're out there. Prostitute women, even more than other women, are always blamed for the social ills and everything that happens in the community. I live in a certain area of town where there has always been poverty, there has always been drugs, and the prostitutes just moved in there. A blind woman was raped the other day, and the prostitutes are being blamed. If the prostitutes weren't in that area, people argue, this wouldn't have happened. I put it back into the lap of the people who are doing this. This violence is the responsibility of the men that are doing it, not of the women that are receiving it. Let's put it into perspective and hold the men accountable for their behaviour.

PARTICIPANT 7: I'm shaking with rage right now. I'm very angry, and I'm offended by your remark about how women dress to provoke and that they deserve what they get.

SUSAN G. COLE: I think everybody interpreted the remark to say that women get dressed in a certain way and provoke rape. I think, if I may try to fill this one out, that the person was remarking that women sometimes dress for themselves or maybe for their own privilege or maybe to please men and that maybe we should be looking at what part we play when we're doing that or, perhaps, contributing to consumer society by spending a gazillion dollars on makeup. Not that women ask for it.

PARTICIPANT 8: I direct my question to Christine Boyle. With the assumption that there's been a change in the law to redefine prostitution as gender-neutral, I question your statements that laws about prostitution are asymmetrical toward women and that there's a legal expression of the subordination of women because it denies that the male prostitute has status. And you mentioned that we should not discriminate *for* sex, but you've discriminated *against* sex and also against sexuality.

CHRISTINE BOYLE: I'm not quite sure that I understand your point. The laws are symmetrical, or at least the trend is toward symmetrical laws, although the enforcement patterns, I think, are quite different, as we've heard very clearly. There's no symmetry in enforcement, and I said there are distortions. I rejected symmetry against a context of distortions of race, class, and sexuality. I think laws have to reflect reality to a certain extent.

The problem I've seen is that the defining of what is deviant reflects, I suppose, a particular class perspective, a particular heterosexual perspective, and a particular male perspective. I don't think we're going to get anywhere by behaving as if all those distortions didn't exist in reality; by believing that there are differences in reality, and just because we've got laws that don't take those into account, think that we've achieved equality. But I don't see that this addresses your point. I don't think we've got very far if we have mutual laws, equally enforced against a real background of divisions of class, sexuality, and gender. But I'm merely repeating my point, and if it's offensive to you, I guess it's offensive to you again ... so I'm sorry.

PARTICIPANT 9: Christine Boyle and Sheila Noonan, I like a lot of what you said, but I'd like to know where in your work you're going to be discussing how racism in pornography contributes to the racial control of people of colour and how it defines the sexuality of people of colour.

SHEILA NOONAN: I want to thank you for posing the question. I think that there really hasn't been enough analysis undertaken of the implications of racism in pornography and how that translates into racial inequality. And I think I can speak for both

Christine and me on this. We're here to learn, and we would appreciate hearing a little more from people and analysis from the inside rather than from the outside.

PARTICIPANT 10: I'm wondering to what extent there is a dialogue going on between the women who are academics and the women who are working in the sex industry. Are there mechanisms existing for such a dialogue?

MARIANA VALVERDE: I don't think there are any formal mechanisms. The links that have been made have happened at the grass-roots level of the women's movement. The dialogue so far has been informal, and we need to integrate what we are learning into our work — not only academics but activists and other women as well.

PARTICIPANT 11 (male): I work with a lot of young people who are involved in the street, and in my experience there are very few of them who make informed decisions about whether they're going to prostitute or not. On the other hand, when I speak to adults who are in the sex trade industry, one has to acknowledge that there are people who may make informed decisions. Is it possible to entertain the idea that an exchange of sex for money isn't always sexual domination? I appreciate that in the current context it is, that it's very dangerous that women are subjected to violence and so on, but is it possible to conceive of a situation where there's an exchange of sex for money in which people give consent? And is there something terribly wrong with that idea?

MARIANA VALVERDE: I think that all these things are often confused: the fact that sex takes place for money, that it takes place without love and without the benefit of a legal marriage, that it takes place either in the street or in bars or something as opposed to in a nice home in the suburbs. All these things get kind of thrown together, and we *do* have to try to separate them. Even though they can't be separate in the real world right now, we should try and analyze them a bit.

I think that it would be quite possible to have an exchange of sex for money that does not involve social relations of domination. It might be more possible among homosexual men because between a man and a woman, you already have all the issues of gender privilege. However, even with homosexual men it tends to be younger boys and older men, and then you do have a power differential. But I would imagine it might be possible to have that kind of exchange for money without all the bad things that go with it in our society. It is a very complicated question because if you exchange sex for money, then you are saying something about the value of sex, and I think that again would need more questioning. We shouldn't assume that just because somebody has sex for money and somebody else has sex for love, one person is better than another person.

SUSAN G. COLE: I'll buy it under two conditions. First of all, let's have perfect economic equality between the sexes so that we're absolutely certain that nobody's going into this business out of economic desperation of any form. Second, I'll buy it if there are as many women buying as there are men, and I'm not sure that's ever going to happen. You may consider that social change, which is fine. At present I find it hard to think about these circumstances as non-subordinating as long as the economic circumstances are the way they are. I find it difficult to avoid noticing who's buying and who's selling.

Racism in Pornography

Lesbians of Colour

We want to look at the particular ways that Women of Colour, Black women, and Native women are represented in pornography. It's important to remember while doing this that all women, excluding white women, are Women of Colour.

How many women or men have not recognized racism in pornography or in advertising? If you think that you have seen racism in pornography or in advertising, how did you know it was racist?

Racism in pornography is not just a matter of having a Woman of Colour portrayed in a picture. Racism is not only in the picture but also in the eyes of the beholder. For example, a woman photographed lounging on a carpet can be clothed in any manner, but when a person looks at the photo and sees a Black woman, all of the stereotypes they have about Black people are operative. So it's not just a woman lying on a carpet.

We can observe definite themes in the use of racial stereotypes. These same themes can be observed in other kinds of imagery that is produced by the media industry. For example, there has been a number of posters advertising Jamaica that feature a photograph of a woman with *Jamaica* emblazoned across her breasts. Those travel posters demonstrate the relationship between what is going on in mainstream advertising and what goes on in pornography. They're making use of the tattoo, which was originally a symbol of women's power. Looking at the history of racism, we note that one of the major ways of identifying slaves, one of the major ways of identifying people in concentration camps, has been the tattoo. This symbol of power has been translated into a symbol of domination, and it is now used this way in the pornography and literature that is produced by the entertainment media.

Most Women of Colour portrayed in pornography appear in one specific, stereotypical image. Black women are usually depicted in a situation of bondage and slavery. The Black woman is shown in a submissive posture, often with two white males. This setting reminds us of all the trappings of slavery: chains, whips, neck braces, wrist clasps. These are the means of keeping Black people in their place.

Another stereotype we have to deal with is the Black man as rapist. It's bad enough being male and not being able to resist a woman, but it's even worse when you're a Black male, because then you've got no hope in hell of stopping yourself!

And the flip side of that coin is how Black women's sexuality is portrayed. If they're saying that about Black men, what are they saying about Black women?

The caption below a photo of an Asian woman in a readily available porn magazine reads, "Japanese girls, who have been subject to many bad jokes, are not built differently from their Caucasian counterparts, and this we have on good authority. The only comment our reporter would make that might cause controversy for the future dealt with the diet. 'Japanese people eat a lot of rice and raw fish,' said our man, 'and this we feel causes the cunt to smell like a barrel of rotten fish.' We didn't ask you to smell it, just look at it." This is a very stereotypical image of Japanese women: they dress in kimonos, eat raw fish and rice, and have no interest in life other than having men smell their cunts. It's a submissive posture, it's a geisha posture, and this is how Asian women are usually portrayed in pornography. Asian women are portrayed in "higher than life" situations, surrounded by palm trees.

One of the pornographic articles I've found involving Native women is entitled "Indian Giver," and it plays on the racist connotation of *indian giver*. The woman is posed as a tease — she promises to give and then takes it back.

Penthouse and *Playboy* do not include Native women. In them you find mostly Black women and Asian women. Native women are more often found in hard-core porn books. I don't know what this really means for Native women. It may be that Native women and Native culture have been so oppressed that the very notion of putting them in these magazines would turn white men off. Native people have been so severely stereotyped as ugly, savage, poor, and drunk that the presentation of their beauty and attractiveness is inconceivable to the producers and consumers of pornography. Pornography exists because somebody buys it, and so it generally caters to the mentality of the white male reader.

The Women of Colour usually displayed in pornography are either Black, Asian, or Latin. It is significant that some Women of Colour are excluded.

Women of Colour struggling against racism have a particular concern with pornography. We don't want pornography; we don't like it because of what it says about our sexuality. It degrades us and makes us out to be either sexual animals or passive creatures. But you can have two pornographic images of women, one a white woman and the other a Woman of Colour, both in the same pose and the same dress, and both of them are being degraded because of their gender. However, for Women of Colour it's not only the sexism, it's also the racism. That is very harmful.

One article in the book *Take Back the Night* points out that stereotypes are, in part, based on the realities of how people have had to adapt themselves in order to deal with oppression. Take the stereotypes of Black people and sex. Black people really are sexy. Historically, our rich and earthy heritage and our relationship to our land allowed us to be more in tune with our bodies. This was quite different from the ways of puritanical Europe. White people encountered something very different and people who were behaving very differently, sexually and socially. Because of their cultural bias they took it to be something very dirty, very degrading, something quite sleazy. These stereotypes are still present today.

Black people, especially Black women, were thought to be the evil side of white people; they had in them the savage, the evil.

PARTICIPANT 1: The same thing happened in South America when the white people came and found that the civilizations were doing all these sexual acts and were also portraying them in their pottery. The Europeans were totally amazed and aghast at the extent of the sexuality of the people of colour in South America and in the Caribbean and in Africa. They wanted to suppress it but at the same time found it exotic because they came from a place where they weren't allowed to express themselves in those kinds of sexual ways. So they ended up being attracted to it, to their "darker" side.

LESBIANS OF COLOUR: In Canada it's safe to talk about racism in a historical framework. The same is true in other countries. But we don't talk about it as being in the present, in Toronto and here at this conference. When you distance yourself from racism, it's easier to deal with because you can think of it as something that happens somewhere else at some other time and ignore what is right on your doorstep.

Issues of race are invisible in the dominant discourse on pornography. I think it's a very serious problem, and it goes to the very heart of the way women are talking about pornography. I didn't realize that the issues of race were so central until I myself started exploring the history of the use of pornography and the oppression of different groups. The first major use of pornography in North America was part of the reaction to the anti-slavery movement in the United States. That was when pornography first became a mass-consumption item in the U.S. Then it was used against Catholics in what was called the "Know Nothing" campaign in the United States, and then it was used against people of Jewish heritage, and so on.

Instead of treating issues of racism as "add-ons" to the analysis of pornography, we should be starting with race because that's where the power of pornography as a method of domination stems from. That's one of the best-kept secrets around. Pornography has a history of being used as a political tool of control. Certainly that has been the case with extreme right-wing states. The Nazi regime used pornography as a tool in the racist portrayal of Jews. It was a very, very important factor in the spread of the stereotypes among the German population. Racism is not an aside.

PARTICIPANT 2 (male): It doesn't necessarily have to be right-wing states. I was in the Canadian army years ago, and we were taught how to castrate. Pornography was part of being in the army. There is a definite sexual component of the army; the drills are all sexual drills. So it's happening here too.

LOC: The whole basis of propaganda is stereotyping your enemy in a very negative way. Pornography is an example of discrimination, whether it be racist, sexist, or classist, used by the ruling apparatus to organize.

PARTICIPANT 3: In the context of the Black struggle in the United States, it's quite apparent that states that sought to eliminate racism on a legal level as well as cultural and economic ones were quite happy to pass anti-defamation laws as one of the main anti-racist initiatives. It was considered a legitimate way to fight racism. But now, even though pornography involves very strong racist stereotypes, the ideology of freedom of speech seems to be given priority. I guess I'm confused or scared about the way in which legal regulations now seem to be so discredited when they were a main tool before.

LOC: It's a very difficult dilemma. It's very difficult, especially for Women of Colour, to try and decide whether we should adopt a strategy of reforms and work for some kind of legislation. I don't hold out very much hope that legislation will have any real short- or long-term effects for us. Meanwhile, though, I have very real concerns. I don't want these men and people who control the media and the profits to go untouched and to get away with all of this. So it's a very real dilemma for us. How do we organize against these people who produce this stuff and make all these profits? I don't know what the solution is. I think the solution lies at the community level, in groups becoming more aware of the exploitation involved in this stuff and working on problems within our communities.

Pornography is not just a battered image; pornography is about whether we have schools or not. It's about whether we are able to have access to jobs or not. These images promote stereotypes that get translated into very real situations. We are faced with stereotypes that Black people are lazy, that West Indians are lazy, that we only like parties, that we only like drinking rum, that we're not capable of organizing a high school, that the kids who come to it are going to steal, loot, and plunder.

PARTICIPANT 4: One of the areas that I find most troublesome for myself is what I see as a conflict between my theory about pornography's role in society and the eradication of pornography and the reality of women's lives. That problem comes most to my mind when I'm confronted by women who are involved in the sex trade. Most of those women are Women of Colour, here and in the States. The conflict, of course, is that those women are saying that we are directly threatening their livelihood, and that's a reality of their lives.

PARTICIPANT 5: I'm a member of a group that's interested in the conversion of military plants. We know that the people working in the plants may not agree with the production of the bombs, but it's their job, it's their livelihood. The workers aren't unionized, and we have to decide whether to help instigate a union or to organize at a plant that is unionized. That may be a useful comparison.

PARTICIPANT 6: That may be an issue of conscience for those people, but those people have other choices. We're talking about women with no jobs until we have an ideal world where there are choices available to all women who don't have to participate in this trade. But this is not an ideal world, and you can't consciousness-raise with Women of Colour who just don't have the choices. I don't mean to sound defeatist — it's just the reality. What alternatives can you give them?

LOC: It's not a question of raising their consciousness. Their consciousness is already raised quite considerably. Historically, the system of oppression created a situation where there weren't very many other choices for Women of Colour. Certainly that's the case today for women in the Third World, where pornography and prostitution are very much related to economic dependence. There is very little else that they can do in order to survive.

The women's movement has to both oppose pornography and support women, just as we support women in low-paying jobs. We support women in low-paying jobs, but we also criticize capitalism. A similar situation has to occur with women involved in the sex trade industries. Their views and what they are about and who they are must be a part of and incorporated into the analysis of what we are facing here. There has not been a lot of analysis coming from the sex trade workers or Women of Colour sex trade workers or Black women sex trade workers. It's a process that's going to take very many years. It's not something that can evolve overnight.

In the short term, what will help the situation considerably is for white feminists, who have the power and the resources, to address themselves very much to what they can do to help the situation.

PARTICIPANT 7: As much as they lobby to get legislation to end pornography, I don't know if there's any group that is collectively trying to find alternatives for these women, especially Women of Colour, who make their livelihood from the sex trade. Although the alternative, for sure, is not going to be as lucrative as the sex trade, without it there is nothing they can turn to without skills or education.

I also think that it's not necessarily up to white women to come in and show these women how to find alternatives for themselves. They'll listen to Women of Colour much more easily than they'll listen to white feminists. Women of Colour can work better in alliance with Women of Colour who are in the sex trade and give them support in a way that the white feminist movement can't.

PARTICIPANT 8: When we look at the power dynamics in society in general, we see that a hierarchical structure exists in a patriarchal, military society. It's all built in there. It's not incidental that there are more Women of Colour involved in pornography. It's all part of the hierarchical system of oppression.

LOC: This conference is supposed to be about challenging our images. However, the lack of representation of Women of Colour on panels and in workshops, and the absence of an integrated anti-racist perspective in the presentations of white women, demonstrate that you really aren't challenging anything. We continuously hear white women say how pornography affects women, but it's clear that they're speaking about white women only; they make Women of Colour invisible because we and racism are not mentioned. The time for white women to include an anti-racist perspective in their dialogue is *long* overdue.

PORNOGRAPHY AND PROSTITUTION IN THE PHILIPPINES

Martha O'Campo

Since the presentation of this piece, the dictatorship of Ferdinand Marcos has been removed. While the dictatorship is gone, the military institutions remain intact, and there has been no significant change in the status of prostitution and pornography in the Philippines. The present government has demonstrated some concern about child prostitution, but improving the situation of women working in the sex trade has not been a priority of the government of Corazon Aquino.

IT IS NECESSARY TO SITUATE prostitution and pornography within the context of the national struggle in the Philippines and also within the context of the women's movement. The Philippines has a population of about fifty-four million people. It has some seven thousand islands and is almost three-quarters the size of California. It has many resources, such as agriculture, fishing, minerals, and also very skilled workers. Apparently it is the second-largest exporter of doctors. Eighty percent of the people live below the poverty line, and 60 percent of the children are malnourished. It is estimated that at the end of 1985 the Philippines will have a $34 billion debt. The average daily wage of a woman in the export-processing zones is eleven to eighteen pesos, which is worth $0.75 to $1.00. The unemployment rate is 40 percent. We can say that at the moment the Philippines is in a state of political, economic, and military crisis. (I will discuss the military a little later.)

There are several reasons why the Filipina woman can play a very decisive role in changing the Philippines to a free and just society. First, the economic participation of women is largely unrecognized and undeveloped because, of the twenty-four million Filipinas, 70 percent are unemployed. The millions of women labouring as unpaid family workers are a vast reserve of productive, but marginal, workers.

Second, industrial and commercial enterprises employ women as cheap labour, profiting from hiring young women and subjecting them to low wages, long hours of work, health hazards, sexual abuse, and union busting. The export-oriented industries purposefully employ women for their submissive character.

Third, the exploitation of women in the flesh market has become aggressive and organized on an unprecedented scale. The use of women as sex commodities ranges from erotic models and child prostitutes to mail-order brides, domestic slaves, and troupes of dancing girls for overseas entertainment.

Fourth, the use of sexual intimidation and terror by the armed forces and its paramilitary units has made women and children the most vulnerable targets in the campaign for suppressing dissent.

With these four categories in mind, I would like to read you a statement made by an electronics worker to emphasize the kinds of sexual exploitation that women are experiencing: "We are aware of management's various ways of trifling with women, both single and married. Sex exploitation is made easy through the appraisal system, which is done every six months. It is when promotions, salary increases, demotions, transfers to other departments, or firings are conducted. If an appraiser happens to like you and you won't accept his invitation for a date, he can rate you lower than your actual performance, and so many women are left with no choice but to accept the date."

Here's another statement, this time from a woman who has become very poetic as a result of her experience on an island in the Philippines: "This place used to be a quiet island. When the tourists started to come, the beach saw new hot-blooded men making it with brown girls, bars blaring loud music, and everyone trying to get a slice of the fun. If you ask these blue-eyed men why they came here, they tell you that the girls serve them like kings in heaven with many docile feminine playmates. If the coral reef were to speak, it would cry about the plunder of our women and their values, the sea becoming polluted, the sky witnessing the ebb of industry, turning kissing into soliciting."

Now I'd like to talk about the American bases in the Philippines and their role in Filipino prostitution and pornography. During the Vietnam war the rest and recreation, often known as "R and R," facilities of Olongapo City (where the Subic Naval Base is situated) became an important part of the recreation and moral appeasement of the Marines. After months of strenuous employment in Indochina, the GIs could relax in the entertainment business of Olongapo, which mushroomed during that time. Even today the Subic Naval Base is regarded by the Marines as a good port because of the cheap and easily available R and R services. With an average of twelve warships in port, roughly seven thousand marines per day seek entertainment in the countless bars, discos, and massage parlours of Olongapo City.

Angeles City, near the Clarke Air Base, also has rest and recreation facilities. About ten thousand registered and unregistered Filipinos work in the rest and recreation business in Olongapo and Angeles cities. The basic characteristic of prostitution in the Philippines is the same in Manila, the smaller cities, and the cities that service the American military bases. Rural poverty drives women to the city. There they are exploited by tour operators, pimps, hotel management, and their customers. The government unofficially, but energetically, encourages the trade.

But there is a poignancy to the prostitution around the American bases that makes it different from other places in the country. In Manila and other large cities prostitutes and hospitality girls look at their work in purely practical terms. Transient tourists do not offer even the illusion of a long-term relationship. But in the cities where the American bases are located, servicemen offer the possibility of marriage, escape from poverty, and the realization of the American Dream. For most of the thirty thousand prostitutes in these areas, marriage to a serviceman remains a dream. Most of these women have babies, called *Amerasian* babies. They end up being abandoned on the street, being sold through adoption agencies, or becoming child prostitutes.

There is no doubt that the rest and recreation industry thrives on the dollar. But what is not obvious is the connection between military buildup, both Filipino and American, and the use of women as sex objects. Visit any military camp in the Philippines, and you'll find women serving as mistresses of draftees, regular and reserve officers, and paramilitary combatants; they are referred to as common-law wives. War and guns make men turn to sex to arrest trauma or to escape from fear and guilt. With their pay envelopes soldiers think they are entitled to liberty, the privilege of using women. With their guns soldiers demand this liberty delivered at their feet.

Now I'll talk about the hospitality girls more in the cities. In the crowded nightclubs in Ermita, the tourist belt in Manila, you'll find beautiful women working very hard; this symbolizes the special burden borne by women and their foreign, Oriental model for economic development. Pushed out of the countryside by poverty, women come to the cities in search of the new jobs offered to them instead of to men. But the opportunities are less than they imagined. There are not enough jobs, and they pay poorly. The major growth industry in countries like the Philippines is tourism, which often demands more of women than their labour.

The procurement of women for pleasure, particularly the pleasure of foreigners, is a multi-tiered system in the Philippines. Open invitations to enjoy the mysteries of a hospitality girl are only the most visible manifestations of a prostitution phenomenon that grows larger with the arrival of each new tourist. *Hospitality* is generally taken to be a euphemism for prostitution because the wages paid by club owners are scarcely livable. The well-known desire of tourists and leisure-class Filipinos for available women provides a substantial source of additional income to the government.

Prostitution in the Philippines has always flourished in places where there is a heavy concentration of foreigners. After the imposition of martial law in 1972, Marcos made the tourist industry such a major priority that it became the fourth largest source of foreign exchange in the late seventies. Because of the present situation, however, tourism is no longer attractive to tourists.

As the nearest wealthy country, Japan provides much of the main tourist business. Twenty-nine percent of all visitors to the Philippines are Japanese, and the tourist industry is particularly accommodating to Japanese men. Prostitutes have been banned in Japan since 1958, and free access to women has long been offered as an inducement to visit the poorer countries of Asia. Because they usually travel in groups, the Japanese are especially conspicuous in their pursuit of women. It has become a familiar sight in Manila to see busloads of Japanese men pull up outside a club, disembark, go inside, and choose a partner for the evening.

Examination of the town of Rajens reveals glaring evidence of the routine exploitation of women by operators who see them as commodities to be assigned and dispensed with in as efficient a manner as possible. Typically, a large Japanese operator will advertise a package tour for the Philippines in co-operation with a Manila agent. The deal will include everything from shopping to accommodation to women, who are either chosen from a particular book in Japan or selected in person in one of the clubs, which will employ about two hundred women during a typical night-life tour.

Sources in the business report that men on tour pay an average of $60 for a night with a woman. Only between $4.25 and $5.25 goes to her; the rest is split among the club owner, tour operator, and Japanese guide. Often the woman does not get even that much because the club management imposes fines for improper dress, smoking, drinking, tardiness, and other arbitrary infractions.

The Philippine government financed the construction of several first-class hotels in Manila to house delegates to conventions such as the International Monetary Fund and the World Bank. According to its own statistics, these hotels have been plagued with occupancy problems. The well-known "joiner-pass" system has been well established, revealing the relationship between the local capitalists and the hospitality industry. One hotel management admitted to making 40 percent of its gross income from the joiner system. Here's what the joiner system is all about.

Women enter the hotel at 5 P.M. through the employees' entrance. They leave at 8 A.M. the next morning. They are not permitted to be taken to any of the public areas of the hotel, and all food and drink orders must be sent by room service. The hotel charges a joiner's fee of $10 for the right to take a woman to a room.

Prostitution is technically illegal in Manila, but apparently hotels operate with complete protection. It is important to add that these are not cheap waterfront dives, but respectable, first-class, government-financed accommodation. It is obvious that the Manila police are involved when one of the several uniformed officers accepts bribes from the women as they leave in the morning. Women report that they have to pay $1.50 each per evening to the police for protection. So for the majority of prostitutes it is a case of being denied access to the goods of society. They have nowhere else to go. Here are the profiles of a few women to give you an idea of where these women are coming from.

Olga is eighteen years old. Her mother took her to work in a bar as a go-go dancer when she was fourteen. Her beauty was regarded as an asset by a family plagued with poverty in Samar. She lost her virginity the first night of her employment at Les Beaux, two years ago. She says, "I am ashamed to work in that place, but I do because of financial reasons."

Gina works on M. H. del Pilar Street in Ermita at the Legs Cocktail Lounge. She's sixteen and has learned how to hustle customers into the lounge, whereas the women at Les Beaux just wait for the Japanese tour buses to arrive. Gina works every night from 5 P.M. to 5 A.M.. She says, "My boyfriend in the province took me and then left. I was ashamed and very poor, so I left with a friend and came here. I send some money to my family. They think I am just a waitress."

Felissa is twenty-eight and single. She's been at Les Beaux for several years. She comes from the Bicol region and is supporting her parents and sending a brother through school with her earnings. She also supports an adopted baby. The adoption was actually a purchase from another hostess for $100. "I didn't want to be lonely, and I didn't want to ruin my body by getting pregnant."

After a time the stories take on a depressing similarity. Poor, young women, usually with tales of being jilted or separated or taken advantage of, feel they have nothing to lose by entering the trade. Codes of sexual morality are strict in the Philippines, and the contrast between the ideals of the seductive mistress and the chaste wife/mother/sister is particularly strong. However, a woman engaging in premarital sex can regain her virtue if she eventually marries her lover. If the relationship ends without marriage, she loses all respectability. The minute women lose their virginity, they feel hopeless. Their ostracism by nearly all sectors of society is a major problem in rehabilitating them. Lost virtue prompts women to turn to prostitution, and the financial rewards encourage them to make it a career. With little education and no vocational training, what else is there? "What else can I do?" asks Felissa.

I would also like to touch on child prostitution in the Philippines. Around the American bases the Amerasian babies are pretty much left abandoned in the streets; some agencies try to have them adopted. They are sent all over the Philippines and to other parts of the world. Around the bases there is really no alternative for these kids because there are no educational or training facilities, nor is there agriculture or industry to keep them employed. So the only alternative is to go into prostitution.

In 1983, for example, an Irish-Catholic priest who was working in a VD clinic in Olongapo City exposed the dirty work of one serviceman. Apparently this fellow had had sexual relationships with twelve young girls aged nine to fourteen. All these girls had stories to tell.

The priest found that these girls were Amerasian. Most or all of them came from very poor families; some had no known male parents or no parents living with them at all. Several of them had been raped by local policemen and subsequently became prostitutes. Others had sold their virginity to American service-men for between $25 and $60; later they received $13 to $20. Most of these girls were infected with VD. After the actions of this serviceman were exposed in the media, the United States let him leave the Philippines. They said that he was already out of the country, so there was nothing much we could do. However, this became a real issue. *Forum*, a newspaper that has been closed by the regime, exposed it quite openly.

As I mentioned earlier, the tourist industry uses pornography to drum up business. For instance, it uses all kinds of erotic and pornographic pictures of women and children to attract Japanese men to come to the industry. That's very popular. But pornography is also used by other industries. In 1983 the Manila International Film Festival ran into great debt. So the government screened a lot of pornographic films to help them raise money. At the time there were also a number of so-called experimental cinemas, which are, in fact, pornographic cinemas headed by Amy Marcos, the daughter of Mr. Marcos. When Imelda Marcos was questioned about this, she said that the media was just making a big fuss. Those were just pornographic films, after all.

I also want to touch on the issue of mail-order brides. These are women who are advertised for marriage by men in other countries. The main problem is that most of these women don't know anything about the culture of the country in which they will live. All they know is that they want to escape from poverty. So when they arrive in North America, their fates really are in the hands of the so-called grooms. Some get lucky and find nice men. But we have also heard of a lot of instances where they are just at the disposal of these men. So they might also be passed on to other agencies or other businesses of prostitution. This is something that is not discussed very often in the media.

Because the Philippines has a $34 billion foreign debt, the export of skilled labourers is very important. But the government is also encouraging the export of Filipino entertainers — meaning exotic female entertainers — all over the world. You hear in the media over and over again about Filipino exotic dancers, even in the Middle East.

To sum up, it is sufficient to state that the flesh market proliferates in the Philippines because of a) the number of tourists paying for sex tours, b) the military buildup and the presence of the American military bases, c) the push of rural and urban poverty, and d) the acceptance of female subjugation.

The women's movement in the Philippines is addressing the issues of pornography and prostitution. GABRIELA, a coalition of organizations of women, is addressing these issues along with all the other issues in the national struggle toward a free Philippines. AWARE (Association of Women Against Repression and Exploitation) offers a program on the sexual exploitation of women. Many religious organizations are just now focusing on the struggles of women. But I want to emphasize that this is only one issue. For instance, the abuses and violent acts of the military are very real problems terrorizing the Filipino people today. Prostitution and pornography are part and parcel of the larger problem that the country has to struggle against if it is to achieve peace and justice.

PART TWO

SEX TRADE
WORKERS SPEAK

HERE ARE THE SELF-PROCLAIMED "bad girls." They are also known as prostitutes, strippers, hookers, dancers, ladies, girls, and whores. Some of these women are longtime advocates of sex trade workers' rights, such as Marie Arrington and Margo St. James. They have a good deal of experience in bringing the issues before the public. Amber Cooke and Mary Johnson are both retired veteran strippers who have remained active in the movement in order to organize women in the sex trade. Valerie Scott and Cathy both work and organize as prostitutes in Toronto, and Scott has been particularly active in promoting dialogue between feminist organizations and prostitutes.

In their presentations and also in their interaction with the conference participants, these women defend, even celebrate, their bad girl identity. They answer criticism of their occupations, speak quite frankly about their work, and passionately express their concern about the impact of the state and the women's movement on their lives. The most controversial claim they make is to the title of feminist as well as bad girl.

One of the major complaints of sex trade workers in Canada is that they have rarely been invited or permitted to speak for themselves in a public forum. In Part Two they do just that.

THE RECLAMATION
OF WHORES

Margo St. James

HOWDY! TI-GRACE ATKINSON ONCE SAID that the women's movement wouldn't really make it over the hump until whores evolved
as the leaders. Well, here we are!

During my twelve years of campaigning for hookers' rights, in
the States and in Western Europe, I've noticed that the women's
movement is quite antsy about prostitution and pornography. It
sees it as a scarlet menace, like the lavender menace when gay
rights were first brought up.

But prostitutes were not always regarded as marginal. In the
Middle Ages in the south of France each little town had its own
"stooge," or public house. They called them hot tubs, baths, and
brothels. Before prostitution was criminalized, there were two
kinds of public baths — one for the non-prostitutes and their
mates and one for the prostitutes and their customers —
sometimes owned by the same woman. In the States between
1907 and 1918 prostitution was primarily a woman-run business.
And then the criminal law was introduced to regulate or control
or supposedly stamp out prostitution, but it didn't really.

The effect of criminalization is that clients are guaranteed a
turnover and a variety, which are what they want. When the

police are licensing, they don't give licences to anyone with a prostitution record. Communities that hope that licensing bawdyhouses will get whores off the street have a false hope because the people with a record aren't allowed to get a licence or get off the street. Only amateurs can get a licence. The police remove the professionals from the business by arresting them. The enforcement is discriminatory, racially and class-wise. It solidifies the dividing of women into good girls and bad girls, and it's an official gender stigma for women, whether it appears neutral at first glance or not.

Prostitution laws have been apparently neutral since the early seventies in the States, but that doesn't mean clients are arrested. Thirty percent of those arrested are men, but only 10 percent of those men are clients. The rest are male prostitutes. And if they are arrested, they're given a citation, and perhaps their names are put in the paper, but they don't do any jail time.

In some states there are mandatory jail terms for women. Prohibition serves to subjugate women, keeping women "one down" or "three down." The whore stigma is attached to women and only to women. I use the word *whore* because I prefer it to *prostitute*. Prostitution can be anything. "Prostitution of one's talents for an unworthy cause" is the definition in the dictionary. I prefer the word *whore*, and I want to reclaim it like lesbians have reclaimed the word *dyke* over the last decade.

In private the whore has power. She is in charge, setting the terms for the sexual exchange and the financial exchange. In public, of course, she has absolutely no rights — no civil rights, no human rights. Prostitution laws are how women are controlled in this society. The great fear for men, who are running things, is that if whores have a voice, suddenly good women are going to find out how much their time is worth and how to ask for the money. I really think that women are being put in jail for asking for money. It's not the sex, because in most states in the U.S. consensual sex between adults is perfectly legal unless you do it on the doorstep. Then, of course, you'll scare horses. But talking about sex is against the law. The courts have said this is not a violation of the prostitute's free speech because her speech is commercial. It's not removing her constitutional right of freedom of association because this is a nuisance and we don't want these people associating or collecting on the corners. Although men have collected on the corners for centuries.

In the Middle Ages, even though prostitutes were considered part of the community, the rape rate was just as high as it is now. And they did not have the slick pornography to generate that kind of abuse. It was in the society. It wasn't present in Florence, Italy, a rich community where women had status, but it was present in the south of France. In Languedoc any woman whose husband had left for a week, or who had abandoned her for good, was fair game. The women who were considered the "priests' good ladies" — maybe these were the lesbians — were fair game. Any woman who didn't have the protection of a man was fair game. And that kind of attitude still persists today because you have to have a man for status.

The government thinks women have to be protected because they can't take care of themselves. I think that attitude perpetuated slavery in the United States too, but we didn't think about reforming the slave, did we? We thought of empowering her or him, and this is what has to happen here.

The state's idea is that these are deviant women and normal men. But they are doing the same thing; they're engaging in the same act. So why should the women be considered deviant because they're separating sex and love? I think separating sex and love is a good thing personally. I think romance may be oppressive. Although I wouldn't recommend being casual these days, unless you're using latex. It's not as safe as it was in the sixties, when I was wildly promiscuous and working as a prostitute. Most women then did not use condoms, although during the last fifteen years every streetwalker with any concern for herself has used condoms for blow jobs and intercourse. Condoms are used more for privacy than for disease and pregnancy control because that's the way prostitutes separate their work from their play.

The scapegoating that's going on today is not new. *Whore* means "unchaste," "defiled," and "diseased." We've got to address those elements and see if there's any fact in those claims. I don't find it. The VD rate among prostitutes has always been lower than among the general public of their own age group — quite a bit lower, in fact, considering that most female prostitutes are between eighteen and twenty-five, particularly on the street. Their rate is 5 percent for VD, but you go into the college campuses, and you find the rate is around 25 percent. If you look at the kids who have been deprived of information about safe sex and taught that it's bad, so they don't take the care that they should, their rate, for the thirteen- to fifteen-year-olds, is 75 percent. So we are under a state rule where pregnancy and disease continue to be used as punishments. I think that we are more enlightened than that. Can't we do something about it?

The division between women is essentially that of good girl/bad girl. It worries me then to hear non-prostitute women use the word *feminist* to refer to themselves and not me. I've always thought that whores were the only emancipated women. We are the only ones who have the absolute right to fuck as many men as men fuck women. In fact we are expected to have many partners a week, the same as any good stud. A woman who has many male lovers is regarded as a whore, whether she's getting paid or not. A man in the same situation is exalted. He's the "Romeo," the "Casanova," and it's okay. We really have to look at how this double standard works and why it hasn't changed, why in fact it's getting worse.

Why are there laws appearing on the books, like C-49, without anybody going down there and making a ripple? Why do those men in Parliament just sail right on through their readings and rubber-stamp it in the Senate? Is it because you all didn't go down there? I think so. The hookers went there, a few people complained, but not enough. Polls show that 60 to 70 percent of the public in the States and Canada feels that the prostitute, the whore, should have the right to work, should have the right to keep her money. Television and magazines have educated the people to the point where they understand the problems that prohibition produces. We saw it in the States with the alcoholic prohibition in the twenties — so much crime, so much violence, hijacking, murders, bombings.

We see it today. Every American city that has proclaimed the loitering law to be valid and ordered street sweeps has seen a serial murderer emerge from the woodwork within a couple of years — Seattle, Portland, Oakland, Los Angeles. Guns are used on prostitutes even here in Toronto. This week a prostitute was killed and left in her hotel room by someone no one knows and who probably won't be caught. In Los Angeles recently the cops finally admitted that there had been a serial murderer on the loose for a year who had murdered ten women, ten prostitutes. The first eight prostitutes were Black women. Nothing was said. The last two were white prostitutes, so it got into the news. But usually it doesn't make the news until a non-prostitute is murdered. And may I say, murderers can't tell who's a prostitute and who's not any more than a customer can. It's their assumption. That kind of violence is generated when any single woman on the street is under suspicion and can be stopped and asked for an explaining of herself. That's what we're working against. We're just losing it if we don't stop these kinds of laws from coming into play.

You can deal with the elements of the crime if you single them out. I'm against the use of the word *pornography* as it is being used today by Catharine MacKinnon and the rest of the theorists and ideologues. Any theory that comes out about prostitution should come from the inside out, not from the outside in; otherwise, it's arbitrary. So when they slide into their "Oh, they're all victims, we must save them!" trip, it supports the continued stigmatizing because it's patronizing and condescending.

Erotica versus porn is a red herring. I want to see porn *not* made synonymous with violence. I want us to see sexually explicit material, period, and separate out the violence. I don't want to see *pimp* used as a characterization of abuse. I want to take the laws that are on the books and go after the people — mostly men — who are using force, fraud, violence, and deceit. The laws needed to do that are on the books already; we don't need special laws to prosecute men who do this to prostitutes.

Prostitution is going on all over. Everybody knows it's a hypocrisy and it's really okay; otherwise, the papers and the phone book wouldn't be advertising it. Guys wouldn't be able to charge it on their credit cards if it wasn't okay. At the same time the victims of abuse continue to be blamed, not protected. Why didn't Linda Lovelace go to the cops when the exploitation was happening? Because she had the whore stigma on her like any porn actor or actress, like any stripper, like any woman who walks the street or works with an escort service.

I think whores need to take steps to protect themselves, not only from physical and legal abuse but also from economic exploitation. There must be some organization that will accept the whores and protect them like they do other performers. Prostitutes are entertainers, let's face it. That's what they are.

Prostitution is by nature a cottage industry. It's something that can be done anywhere, by anyone, and this is what bothers the government. I think they wonder how they're going to get their piece. I don't think it is necessary to set up a bureaucracy to collect the tax, or count the towels, or count the condoms. If a neighbour knows what's going on and thinks the woman isn't paying taxes, he or she will report her. I think that'll take care of itself.

My last word is: please, try not to let the government interfere in this common market. Keep the issue of necessary support services for kids separate from the rights of whores to do their jobs.

UNVEILING

Cathy

I COULD TALK FOR HOURS — the issues are broad, deep, fast, and complex. First I will tell you a little bit about who I am, and then, out of a multitude of issues that could and should be addressed, I've selected a few of the most serious and most urgent issues of concern to sex trade workers and to you as well — to all of us.

Cathy is not my real name. I've always worked as a prostitute under my real name because I've never been particularly ashamed of being a prostitute. But over the last year or so I have ventured out more and more into the public and dealt with the media, and so I've had to use a pseudonym. By now I've got used to *Cathy*, so if you say "Cathy," I'll turn my head.

As far as how I look, Cathy is all right, I can live with Cathy. But wearing a veil is another story. When I go to the Eaton Centre, to the 7-Eleven store, or I'm out and about in my neighbourhood, I don't look like this. I don't really feel good about looking like this now, but in my reality it's a necessity. And I feel I should tell you why. I'm protecting myself —not as you might think, not from the police. I'm really protecting myself from you. In a sense from you, from my neighbours, from my friends who don't know that I'm a prostitute. I am protecting the straight business I also happen to own and operate and that deals as well with the public. This veil is a necessity. I have many friends who have worked very hard around this conference who feel they can't come to it and make a statement about being a sex trade worker even to this extent. They're out there among you as members of the audience. You don't know who they are, and that's a very sad thing.

One of the reasons I am so heavily veiled is that I am the most indictable person sitting at this table. I own and operate escort services. I also work as a prostitute. Being a prostitute is not illegal. Living on the avails of another's prostitution is illegal. Directing prostitutes is illegal. Driving a prostitute to a call is illegal. I have to protect myself. I will do no one any good whatsoever if I am sitting out at the West End Detention Centre.

Some of us have had very brutal experiences in the last year sitting at community meetings of irate citizens who want the prostitutes off their streets. We've sat not with veils, but as ourselves, not being able to say a word. When we weren't busy hiding our faces from the media, we had to deal with the man in front of us who felt that we should be dealt with, with baseball bats. To that we could not say a word. We are silenced, unable to defend ourselves at public gatherings.

I'm not a member of any organization, but that doesn't mean that I stand altogether alone. Within the escort services, going back as far as I can remember, there has always been an attitude of friendliness and co-operation. Although these days, these last two years, as we become bigger and bigger and our phone bills get higher and higher and our safety is more and more threatened, that spirit of co-operation is strained just by sheer physical realities.

Many of us dealt closely but very, very carefully with the Ontario researcher, commissioned by the department of justice, for the Fraser report. He points out that absolutely every escort and escort service owner that he talked to, 100 percent of them, expressed a desire to communicate with the "dominant culture." Among the street girls it was around 95 percent. Unfortunately, because of how it is between us, very seldom are we allowed to address you directly. This conference is exciting because we're here. I can walk down, we can talk.

On one level I regret that I am speaking about escort services and wish, in a sense, that I didn't feel this need to come here and do so, because for years we in the escort services have enjoyed a certain elite position. Although on the books the owners are the most indictable, we've been the best tolerated by the culture. But times are changing. There are more and more escorts, and there are more and more girls on the street, and there are more and more girls in the bars, and there are more and more people out there wanting to stab us thirty-two times. Although I regret drawing attention to the escort services, which have enjoyed that tolerance as we go tiptoeing around in the night, not bothering communities because we're not standing in people's front yards, I feel that there are overriding concerns that affect all of us in the sex trade. And I think we're all going to have to look at making more effort to stand together and help one another out.

Valerie Scott, Marie Arrington, Peggy Miller, and I went to Ottawa and appeared before Members of Parliament, who allowed us to tell them what we thought about Bill C-49. That bill had gone through two readings before I even heard about it. It was nice to go to Ottawa and do that. I don't know what good it did us, but it was nice to go there. Marie could get up on the one hand and talk about twelve-year-olds giving blow jobs in exchange for a sniff of glue, and I, as an escort service owner (and of course all escorts, as we know, drive Mercedes-Benzes and wear fur coats), could speak from my experience. It was very nice to have an opportunity to try to stand together and say to the culture, "We can do this, and we can work together, and many of us have every intention of doing so."

We always have this double-sided thing. On the one hand you have, "Wasn't it great that we got to go to Ottawa?!" It was the first time in history that Parliament had invited prostitutes to walk right in there and say, "Here's what we want." That's wonderful. A month later the bill was passed anyway. Right now the strategy is basically for expediency — to get the girls off the street. Later it's going to be expanded, and the net is going to be drawn in, in another direction — toward the escort services.

We have different women in the sex trade and different laws that apply to them. If I am an escort service owner, I have a whole set of laws here. If I'm a street girl, they're over here. I cringe to think of what C-49 is going to do to us before it's finished, because very few of us are going to stop working. Many of us like to work. It's our choice. Remember that prostitution is legal. The way the laws have been written so far, it's legal to be a prostitute. It's just illegal to do absolutely anything else around it. Everything around it is illegal. It is exactly as though the government is saying to us, "Here, you can buy a new car. You can drive this car anywhere you want to. Take it anywhere, anytime. But you can't turn on the ignition." My greatest concern is definitely about Bill C-49 and what it's going to do to us all. It is a very, very destructive bill, and I believe that from it, down the road, members of our community, our sisters in the sex trade — some of us are going to die because of this bill. I really think we have to work together to have a close look at it, to organize, to resist it, to fight it.

STRIPPING: WHO CALLS THE TUNE?

Amber Cooke

As a life skills coach for the past year, I have been dealing with women who are within the context of the subculture of the sex trade industry and who are trying to understand the larger mainstream culture. I have not been dealing with reform, that is, convincing women that what they are doing is wrong and training them to conform to mainstream culture. That doesn't empower women at all. Within their job situations they are individual and creative women, and one of the compromises that strippers make in choosing this occupation, and participating in a job environment where they can be individual and independent, is the loss of protection. They lose the protection of the mainstream legal system. They are women, but they do not have the protection that other women in the workforce do.

The oppressive sexuality that we all know exists, exists for good reasons. There's a tremendous amount of power in sexuality. I believe that mainstream culture is aware of this and fears it.

In the late sixties nudity in entertainment came to Toronto. It was not the burlesque theatres that started the trend. There the dancers wore G-strings and had sticky adornments called pasties attached to their nipples. Bars had not yet discovered that strippers would indirectly sell booze. No. Total nudity came full-blown to Toronto in the gracious Royal Alexandra Theatre. The show had to be a proven success on Broadway before anyone in Toronto dared touch it.

The musical *Hair* had been publicized in every conceivable periodical in the United States. Toronto, in spite of its Presbyterian background, was a city of the world. Nudity at that stage of our development was a reasonably safe bet in the middle- to upper-class environment of the stately lady of King Street. It may be of interest to note that the money required to produce *Hair* came from the Eatons, the Bassetts, and the Mirvishes. These families represented the cream of Toronto acceptability. Any morality officer would think twice before laying charges on any of them.

The owner of the Burlesque theatre on Spadina Avenue decided to take a chance. The Burlesque had a long and saucy history of nudity. What had been available for some years in American magazines could be seen in the flesh and by chaps who carried lunchpails to work. Then Le Strip and, after it, Starvin' Marvin's, opened on Yonge Street. There were many theatres for the presentation of exotic dancing. The old burlesque comedy sketches died a slow and painful death at the Victory. Immigrant-dominated audiences preferred non-verbal communication. The Victory burlesque theatre finally went the way of the old Casino theatre and the Lux before it. Bars by this time had started moving from go-go girls in gong shows to strippers. However, the Liquor Control Board of Ontario exercised strict control over entertainment policies. Total nudity was not permitted. The G-string had to remain firmly in place.

As Ontario bars introduced strippers, certain theatrical productions in Toronto introduced nudity at what is often called the underground or alternative theatres. Toronto Free Theatre, Theatre Passe Muraille, and even the Toronto Dance Theatre, in productions at the St. Lawrence Centre, made liberal use of complete nudity. Morality officers laid charges, but the theatrical community closed ranks. Judges were sympathetic to artistic aspirations, and alcohol was not involved.

Then a seemingly dissociated event occurred. In Sault Ste. Marie Maclean and Maclean, two comics with a penchant for the outrageous, were arrested because of the content of their show in a bar. Nudity was not the issue in this particular case. The judge's decision, however, suggested that the Liquor Control Board of Ontario should have no jurisdiction over what was allowed or not allowed, by way of entertainment, in places selling liquor. Bar owners saw this as a way of ridding themselves of mouthy comics and temperamental rock groups who might walk out if their demands were not met. In a very short time there was nude dancing all over Toronto, all over Ontario. Individual girls were very easy to control. They had no union as did the pesky musicians. When you were employing several girls, one intransigent dancer didn't matter; she could be replaced. In many ways the staid, conservative old province of Ontario became somewhat racy overnight.

In the seventies bodyrub parlours became predominant in Toronto. This was not the bar scene, and it certainly was not theatre. It was not fantasy — it was reality. The rank-and-file stripper considered herself to be in show business, but bodyrub attendants were selling real sex. To be sure, a small percentage of strippers had always turned tricks, but the vast majority are very concerned with their private dignity, probably because so much of society thinks that they lack public dignity. The bodyrub parlours became more visible as trade became more competitive.

Toronto's main drag, Yonge Street, had never been all that glamorous, but at this time it resembled a circus. It was a street we loved to hate. People given to bouts of righteous indignation could point their finger of scorn. Many Torontonians enjoyed being tempted, and a sufficient number patronized a flourishing bawdyhouse industry in the name of massage. Most people felt a little sad about the look of our main street. Is this what Toronto was all about? Then something vicious happened. A young boy, Emanuel Jacques, was killed in a tragic, sadomasochistic, homosexual orgy that took place in a bodyrub parlour on Yonge Street. One employee was at least indirectly involved. The ranks of the righteously indignant grew several thousandfold after reading a single newspaper headline. It is not surprising that the Toronto police could stage a raid on a sadomasochistically oriented homosexual club called the Barracks shortly after the killing of Emanuel Jacques. To much of the general public what was happening was all sexual — whether homosexual or heterosexual, it didn't matter. Yonge Street was cast as a great canyon of perversity. The statistical likelihood of this happening again was of no consideration. The fact that a similar scene had taken place at the old Ford Hotel, when Toronto was as puritanical a city as you could find on the continent, did not matter.

The city fathers devised a plan. It was the standard bureaucratic device of licensing someone out of existence, or nearly so. The category of "adult entertainment parlour" was invented, and along with it the adult entertainer parlour attendant. A parlour licence cost in excess of $3,000 per year. An attendant had to pay over $51 for the privilege of being able to work within Metropolitan Toronto. That's now gone up to $61. What had the exotic dancers to do with the Emanuel Jacques murder? For that matter, what did they have to do with the bodyrubs? A lot of well-intentioned legislation was created, but the street-level sociology was totally ignored. Exotic dancers and bodyrub attendants were lumped into the same category. The dancers were shocked.

The fledgling Canadian Association of Burlesque Entertainers (CABE) was a too-hurried attempt at forming a union. It objected formally. What about freedom of expression? ACTRA, the union for performers in radio, TV, and film, gave some support to CABE, but the issue came more directly under the jurisdiction of the

Union of Stage Actors and Dancers. Actors' Equity appeared not to be interested. By tradition strippers had been represented by the American Guild of Variety Artists. Unfortunately, that union had closed its Toronto office years before. The girls had no effective representation. The Canadian Association of Burlesque Entertainers represented a small fraction of the dancers. It could not act from a position of strength.

In its favour, City Hall did accept a delegation from CABE. The union's initial position was that the dancers should not have to be licensed. The city's representatives asked what particular objection CABE had to the licensing by-law. One clause particularly infuriated the girls. It had to do with getting a doctor's certificate stating that the applicant did not have venereal disease. The by-law people admitted that the implication of this clause was a bit heavy and eliminated it. They said, "We've given you the clause, now you have to give us something." They further argued that a licence would give the dancers professional credibility. The argument for freedom from government control was lost. Licensing was instituted. Now women have to submit a passport photo, indicate any criminal record, and pay $61 to be able to strip in Toronto for a year. The benefit of the licence stops there.

When licensing started, several strippers who had been dancing for years were frightened to apply for a licence because of their records. Presumably some had records for prostitution. Some doubtlessly returned to prostitution rather than have their records revealed.

Bars with a strip policy and a striptease theatre were also required to get licences — to the tune of $3,000 plus per year. Before licensing, there were more than 260 places where dancers could find employment. Some of the smaller places only hired one, two, or three dancers per week, but some of the larger spots hired as many as twenty-eight. The exorbitant cost of the licence, plus the fact that the club owner had to apply in person and show himself to be of upright character, drastically reduced the number of places where dancers could work. There are presently [1985] sixty-two bars and one striptease theatre where exotic dancers can find employment. This is less than a quarter of the number before licensing.

The fee of $3,000 per year for an adult entertainment parlour licence seems punishing, but if your place is big enough, it is not too bad. In fact, the high cost can be a distinct advantage. It keeps out the small-fry competitor. With all the excess dancers available it becomes a buyer's market. Bar owners have cut dancers' salaries, forcing the girls to seek lost income elsewhere.

This brings us to the subject of table-dancing. Three or four years ago table-dancing was introduced to Ontario from Quebec. The dancers are provided with a small table-like platform. They circulate through the bar, set up in front of anyone who will pay the usual $5 per musical number, and strip for them. The dancers initially greeted the trend as a pleasant release from the boredom of unattractive, cold dressing rooms. They could do something between their turns on stage. It meant extra money. It was voluntary.

Soon the problems of table-dancing predicted by older dancers, who had been accused of "old fogeyism," started to show. Club owners started demanding that the girls circulate constantly. Fines were levied against the unco-operative. Ambitious, greedy, and just plain hungry dancers started free-lancing. They got permission from club owners to be allowed to circulate without the benefits of being properly contracted and properly paid. Competition for employment in Metro is high. Club managers know it and readily take advantage of the free talent. The situation has now deteriorated to the point where some of the bars are charging the girls for the privilege of table-dancing. So much for the minimum wage law in Ontario.

Patrons in most striptease bars are usually young and somewhat boisterous men. They tend to come in groups of three to seven and often chip in for a table-dance. In a bar seating a hundred patrons there are as many as thirty-eight women dancing. This sets up a highly competitive atmosphere in which the women are forced to encourage hands-on entertainment, rather than dance, in order to make their money. For most girls this is dangerous. Even if there is a bouncer in the club's employ, he can't watch ten table-dancers at once. He's going to be very reluctant to back up a girl against a table of husky young men. At the non-alcoholic places left, between four and five patrons per year are kicked out for grabbing the women where they have no right. Many individuals have that much trouble on the weekends, and very seldom are the patrons ejected.

To add insult to the already stated injuries, a judge ruled in October 1985 that the one decent clause in the otherwise retrogressive Metropolitan Toronto by-law was invalid. He saw no reason why a dancer should not remove her G-string in a public bar. Immediately the problems of dancers were increased yet again. A few of the women are basking in the financial sunlight of this increased demand; most are greatly saddened and upset by this turn of events. The Supreme Court set this case as a precedent, and it can be overturned at any time by the attorney general. Should the constituents decide to complain that there are nude women on their streets, they simply need to seek approval from the attorney general, and overnight all those women are sitting ducks. They can be busted for obscenity and indecent acts. The maximum fine is $500, and they can get up to two years' probation. Probation means that they cannot enter a licensed premise. They lose their livelihood for two years.

The community of exotic dancers in Toronto is large and scattered. The girls only come together in bars where management discourages any talk of organization. At one end of the social spectrum some strippers are graduates of universities and the ballet school. Some of the women have learning disabilities. You have women who, because of highly restrictive parents or religious upbringing, are making a statement by their choice of occupation. For some it's a very good dollar.

At the other end of the spectrum we have women who were born into alcoholic and/or drug-addicted families, who were pushed from pillar to post, and they are doing the most dignified thing that they will ever do in their lives. They're in show business, they have status, they have a career. A lot of the women have a temporary attitude toward their job. They feel that in six months to a year they will be doing something else, so why be concerned? For these women it is a waste of energy to organize for proper legal rights. The more immediate concerns of preserving relationships and nurturing in your own back yard are considered higher priorities than the vague legal jungle of justice and rights.

Licensing admittedly proved successful in ridding the city of the abuses of the bodyrub parlour, but it was overkill to include exotic dancers. For those bar owners who had licences and had large enough places to capitalize on it, licensing was very good indeed. However, the negative effects of table-dancing and the G-string law are so considerable that they outweigh any short-term financial gain.

When there's a separation between the performer and the audience, it is easier to separate reality from fantasy.

C-49: A New Wave of Oppression

Valerie Scott

I AM WITH THE Canadian Organization for the Rights of Prostitutes (CORP). I am a prostitute myself. I would like to address Bill C-49, which went through third reading in the House of Commmons on November 21, 1985. Every woman should be outraged by this bill. It denies not only prostitutes but also all women free access to their city and freedom of association. It says that "every person, who, in a public place or in any place open to public view, stops or attempts to stop any person or in any manner communicates or attempts to communicate with any person for the purpose of engaging in prostitution or of obtaining the services of a prostitute is guilty of an offence punishable on summary conviction."

It's up to the police to decide what is prostitution. Flagging a taxi may be prostitution. Talking to a friend on the street may be prostitution. The police decide, and we all know they lie in court. Society will not be allowed to communicate with us. We will no longer be allowed to communicate with society. We will be under special scrutiny as soon as we step outside our door. Walking to the grocery store, we can be charged. The police say, "That's taking it a little too far. We won't charge you for going to the grocery store." Maybe they won't, but they have the power to. Also with this bill there will be massive arrests on the street. We will be put through the revolving door once again. The maximum fine will be $2,000 and/or six months in jail. So this will also cost taxpayers a lot of money to process. We'll be back out on the street, only this time we'll have criminal records, that's all. It's not going to stop prostitution, believe me.

We hope that Bill C-49 will eventually be challenged in the Supreme Court and will not hold up. This is just a sham. In 1978 a woman did take the prostitution law to the Supreme Court, and the judge said, "In Canada it is legal to be a prostitute. How can we possibly convict this woman for practising her profession?" That's when it became necessary to be "pressing and persistent" in order to be arrested. It is still legal to be a prostitute in Canada; it's just not legal to do it.

We would like to see all these silly laws thrown away, and for once we would like to see the government deal with prostitution in a grown-up way. The only way to go is to decriminalize prostitution. Decriminalization will enable us to work in many different ways. We'll be able to advertise. We won't have to worry about putting ads in the Yellow Pages or in the papers. We will not necessarily have to be on the street. You would see a mass exodus from street prostitution if women could check into a brothel, if I could work out of my own home, if I had other avenues open to me.

But I want to say — and it is important that you know this — it is our *right* to work on the street. We are allowed to be there just like you are allowed to be there or anyone selling whatever they're selling is allowed to be there. Just because we're prostitutes is no reason to kick us off the street.

I know a lot of people are offended by the sight of prostitutes. They don't like the way we look. They say that we yell and scream on the street. Some of us do. Some people who work with computers are unruly as well. There are laws on the books to deal with this. It's illegal to create a disturbance or be a nuisance in a public place; however, the police are choosing not to use these laws. They are letting the unruly ones create this kind of scene so that the citizens get very upset. The citizens band together and lobby the government. The spineless government ends up passing a bill like C-49. So the citizens have done all the lobbying for the police. They've done all the work for those cops and played right into their hands. They've given the cops unlimited power, and the cops can charge you just like they can charge us under this bill. It's bad for all people. It's sad too. It's really sad that in 1985 this bill could be passed in Canada.

I would also like to address the procuring laws, that is, the laws pertaining to those associated in some way with prostitutes. This is a touchy issue, but a very important one. We would like to see all the procuring laws wiped off the books. This is not to say we're inviting a bunch of pimps to come and run our lives, however; the procuring laws do not apply only to pimps. If I call another girl in the business and give her a date that I have, whether to help her out or because I can't do it, I can be charged with directing a female. This also prevents us from organizing, prevents us from communicating with each other, prevents us from setting up a network to protect ourselves, prevents us from telling each other about bad tricks. We're not allowed to communicate with each other.

A pimp is defined as a person who lives wholly or in part on the earnings of a prostitute. Evidence that a person lives with or is habitually in the company of a prostitute is, in the absence of evidence to the contrary, accepted as proof that the person lives on the avails of prostitution. According to this I'm not allowed to have a boyfriend now because any man who is habitually in my company is defined by the law as a pimp. I'm not allowed to get married. My husband could be charged. We want the procuring laws removed. We demand the right to have lovers.

If prostitution was decriminalized and a pimp did show up at my door, I would be able to pick up the phone and call the police, and they would be able to charge him with extortion or coercion. I can't do that now, or I'll be charged with prostitution. You see how they get you? That's why we must have decriminalization. We can't be oppressed any more. We wouldn't have half as much violence if we could network and protect ourselves and be protected by the law, instead of exploited by the law. I would like your co-operation and your help. Please don't ostracize us anymore. We won't ostracize you either.

COMMUNITY ORGANIZING

Marie Arrington

PEOPLE OFTEN ASK US, "Isn't it true that it's impossible to organize prostitutes? They aren't aware of what's going on, right?" Wrong. I have never met a more politicized group of women. The only difference is that they don't have the power to organize because they are ostracized by the rest of society and threatened by the police. So it has been very difficult, but not impossible, because there are prostitutes' rights groups throughout the world, and more and more are forming all the time.

I'd like to talk a little bit about organizing within the Vancouver community. In the early eighties residents in the west end of Vancouver began to organize against prostitutes on the street. Some of us who are concerned about prostitutes started going to the community meetings and trying to be heard. But of course we were met with tomatoes, eggs, and bottles of beer.

The people organizing with the most strength against prostitutes in the very beginning were gay men, the people that were unacceptable to society not so long ago. That split the gay community wide open because we approached the gay community and said, "Listen, what's going on? There are gay men that are working on the street, and by putting on pressure you are, in fact, putting these people in danger as well as the women. And of all people you should be most aware." It remains a split community. The gay men that were organizing against the prostitutes were the men that all of a sudden had acquired acceptability, having acquired property and good jobs. They aligned themselves with the right wing and the residents. We predicted that these same men would, once this was over, run for political office, which in fact they did. Incredibly, not one of them got in. The gay men who did try to talk about the rights of prostitutes to work, the freedom of association, were pretty well ostracized themselves and were not deemed acceptable anymore.

We also tried very hard to organize within the feminist community. I had been a member of the feminist community for years, but when we started the Association for the Safety of Prostitutes (ASP), we were suddenly ostracized by the feminist community because one of the founders was a whore. I would go to collective meetings and be criticized constantly for my language. I could not say "bitch" because it was misogynist. Women from my collective criticized me and told me that I should be telling the women to get off the street because it was dangerous. The women already knew it was dangerous. They told me to talk to the women and tell them not to use *cunt* and *whore* because they were misogynist. We were telling these women that language was not the priority. The priorities were safety and the right to work. Needless to say, I am not an accepted member of many parts of the feminist community in Vancouver. Many women that I organized with very closely in the past now walk past me.

This is not to say that all feminists are the same, but the media picks up on the sensationalist stuff from feminists, prints it, and then gives the idea to the women on the street that all feminists are against them. When you hear what we call academic pimps get up on TV or in the newspaper, it scares the hell out of the women. They ask us, "What the hell are they talking about? We never did anything to them. Why are they against us?" But the fact is that there aren't enough loud voices within the feminist community, and the ones that are the loudest are the ones that are the most unacceptable to the women on the street.

In Vancouver the 1985 Take Back the Night march was organized to go through the "track." I asked the women on the street if anyone had asked them if they wanted people marching through the track. No one had. They went out there with their placards and their banners, and they went right through the track during the hours when the women were working. They did not tell the women that they were coming down to talk about violence against women, that they were going to be coming through during peak hours of operation. They never asked, "Can we do this?" They just went and did it. One more time it gives the impression that the women in the sex industry aren't important and their opinion doesn't count and their lives aren't acceptable.

Feminists across this country, as well as in the United States, have also organized tours through the sex shops. Many of the women who work in those sex shops say there is nothing more intimidating or degrading than to see a bunch of women sitting in the audience, talking about them as they're up there dancing or performing. It is next to impossible to get these women to stop doing this and to realize what it means to the women that are working within that industry. We have been asking the women, wherever we have travelled, when you're talking about pornography, don't do your tours. You don't need to go through those shops to know what pornography is about. You don't need to intimidate the women within that industry anymore.

In Vancouver we had a Hooker Pride march and rally about three years ago. We had asked the women from the feminist community to please come with us, and many of them did show up. Afterwards we asked these women how they had felt walking through the streets with prostitutes. One of them said, "I was really uncomfortable because I'm not used to walking with women that are half nude." What's the difference between women in shorts that are working on the street and women in shorts that aren't working on the street? In fact, there is no difference. But it is an example of how women who are not prostitutes view hookers differently.

We have organized marches and rallies when hookers have been murdered, and usually it is the street people, the extremely poor people, as well as the women in the sex industry, that show up. It is extremely discouraging. We don't have difficulty organizing on the street or in poor communities. But we find it incredibly hard to organize in the middle-class communities and in the feminist community, I'm sorry to say. This is painful because we should be able to expect support from these areas.

In 1984 prostitutes occupied a church. The provincial government had passed an injunction forbidding all street people, and prostitutes especially, to be in the west end of Vancouver. They could not work in that area. That injunction is still in effect. Women have been charged under that injunction, but we don't know what will happen until the appeals go through. We're trying to have it overturned. It called for an automatic $2,000 fine or two years in jail. So we occupied the church to shed light on the fact that since the injunction had been passed, women had been murdered, and other women had been incarcerated on all kinds of false pretences. Violence against prostitutes had increased dramatically.

Education was part of the four-day occupation. We stayed in the church and had a good deal of dialogue with the community and the church members. A lot of our financial support has come from the Anglican church. I don't know if it's significant or not that all the occupations that have happened so far have been in Anglican churches, but we have made incredible breakthroughs with the church and with organizing people in that community. We have also made breakthroughs with the people in the skid-row areas of the community. They all realize that street prostitution is mainly an economic issue, if not totally an economic issue.

People on the street are the poorest of all people because of government bureaucracy and patriarchy. I've heard the word *patriarchy* used quite a few times this weekend. People on the street don't understand patriarchy, they just know about "the man." And I understand it's the same thing.

We are organizing. We are fighting very hard. We would like to make contact with women lawyers who are willing to do free work to fight Bill C-49. We need to organize throughout this country so that women and men will put their bodies on the line or write letters. Or when you're out on the street and you see a woman working, just nod to her and say, "Hi! How are you?"

CABE AND STRIPPERS: A DELICATE UNION

Mary Johnson

I AM THE FORMER PRESIDENT of the Canadian Association of Burlesque Entertainers (CABE), Local 1689 of the Canadian Labour Congress. The union is not in effect any longer — it died about four years ago — but we were quite active during the time that the Metro Licensing Commission decided to license burlesque entertainers. I'd like to speak a little bit about that because if people get their way, I think the day will come when we'll see prostitutes licensed in the same fashion. This is probably the worst thing that could ever happen to any of us. It certainly has been one of the worst things that has ever happened to the dancers.

The licensing by-law was passed in conjunction with a zoning by-law. A map was passed out to all the aldermen in Toronto and they were asked to please designate which areas of Metro they thought would be all right to have adult entertainment parlours. The map came back indicating that no alderman saw fit to have burlesque entertainers licensed anywhere in Metro Toronto. The licensing by-law does not have the power to legislate an industry out of existence, but this zoning by-law, in effect, does exactly that.

The law was, of course, passed, and we have been licensed for quite some time now. I happen to know that since being licensed, the dancers are all listed with the police, throughout Canada and throughout the world. It is a listing that cites us as criminals. We're not written down as having a criminal record, but we are listed as being strippers. Wherever we go for the rest of our lives, it is on record that we have been strippers. You can understand just how that would taint a person's future, how that would be something that we would never be able to get away from.

The licensing by-law was supposed to help protect the dancer, or at least that's what they said publicly. In fact, practically none of the provisions of the licensing by-law have ever really been enforced, certainly not any of the ones that protect the dancers. There was a time when they wanted our real names and addresses to be posted on every barroom wall where we were. I'm sure you can understand what kind of flack we would get from customers if they were to know where we lived. We made deputations to Metro Council and managed to use stage names on our licences and get that through. But we got very little apart from that.

Slowly but surely a lot of the clubs that have been in existence have started to lose their licences. This has been the downfall of the industry. Table-dancing has come in, the level of professionalism has dropped substantially, and a lot of women who were dancers, because of criminal records, are not allowed to be dancers anymore. This forces them to go into other types of employment, and I hesitate to say that it forces them to become prostitutes, but many of the people who were artists, who were dancers, are now doing other things. And I wouldn't say that they were necessarily into better forms of employment. It has really ruined our industry.

If prostitution were to be legalized, the government would be able to enforce these kinds of controls over prostitutes. The only persons who would really be harmed by this legislation would be the women themselves. It's really something to think about. One of the other issues that the union tried to address was the G-string, or nudity, laws. I really don't have anything against nudity, but I do have something against dancers being the only ones prosecuted for an act of nudity in a club, especially when that act of nudity is a condition of employment. It can be argued that there's a lot of competition and that a club owner is not able to keep up if his dancers aren't nude and the competitor's dancers down the street are. Just the same, I don't see why we should have to sacrifice our women for their competition and to put more money into their pockets. God knows we were never paid any more for dancing nude.

So the union started to fight against nudity. Nudity is governed under Section 170 of the Criminal Code. This section allows punishment on summary conviction, and no proceedings can commence under the section without the consent of the attorney general. Now that sounds all well and good, but if you think about it, when would the attorney general give his consent? I can tell you it is at election time, when they have reason to want to gain the support of the public by their colossal efforts to clean those wanton women off the streets. They would round up the women and arrest them, charge them for nudity in a public place, tell them that they were offending public decency and order, and perhaps win their election campaign. A few months later people in the same place would be going nude, and no charges would be laid because the attorney general would decline to give consent for whatever period. So we never knew what was going to be lowered and when we were going to be arrested. It was a haphazard, selective enforcement advantageous to whoever was in power or hoped to be in power. As a result, many of our women were unjustly prosecuted.

We asked for a clear definition of the law simply to know where we stood — to either have the G-strings on or off, to either have nudity legal or illegal. We were denied this by the attorney general's office. We were told by Attorney General Roy

McMurtry that the police would continue the manner of enforcement that they had always used. Next we went to Metro Council, and we had a section written into the by-law stating that, in accordance with the Criminal Code, in order to be considered not nude in a public place, a G-string of opaque material must be placed over the pubic area. This law has recently been overturned by the Supreme Court.

For a long time many dancers wanted to be nude in a public place or didn't really think that this was an area of contention. But for a long time they were able to perform without the fear of prosecution because the law was clearly defined. And now again we have gone back into the realm of the ambiguous: whenever they want to give their consent for prosecution, we can be prosecuted. We're no longer protected by that provision of the Metro by-law. I might also point out that the law is not concerned with just anyone in a public place who is nude; it is concerned simply with adult entertainment parlour people who are nude in a public place. If the Art Gallery of Ontario decides to have nudes, that's okay. If Theatre Passe Muraille or the St. Lawrence Centre or Basin Street have people nude in a public place, that seems to be okay. Why is it okay? They say that they are covered under the Theatres Act. The Theatres Act, in fact, does not cover them. The Theatres Act covers movie houses.

There are a lot of discrepancies in this law, and it's a very blatant prejudice against people in our industry. We've had no support from any other outside group, including other women's groups. Any progress we've made in this area was while the union was in effect, and at that time there was nothing else being done. These problems still exist today. The working conditions are still as bad as they ever were, and in fact, in many cases worse than they were. Unfortunately, though, today there's no organization to back dancers up.

If there's anything that we would, as sex trade workers, like to ask all of you, it is please, in the future, when you hear of things like this, if you can, take an active part in trying to get the legislation being written to be clear, be concise, be fair, and not be discriminatory toward the women that are working in these industries. Try, maybe for the first time, to service these women, to understand their needs and their problems, to care, and to do something. And when you go to your different unions or your different groups, speak about the discrepancies that there are in the law, and let our voice be heard where it needs to be heard.

FROM THE FLOOR

PARTICIPANT 1: PROSTITUTES are politicized in an entirely different language, but nevertheless we know the issues.

Don't pretend you're interested in our politics if you're only pimping us. I've been out all my life, and I never took a pimp. I'll be damned if a political organization is going to pimp me or any other whore for their agenda. Whores' organizations belong to whores. Because we're very hard to politicize as a group, we're a bunch of mavericks, a number of outside groups have come in and tried to help in our politicization. Ultimately they end up attaching a lot of their own agenda, which means they redefine our issues for us. For instance, Wages for Housework say that if they attach their agenda to ours, they're going to empower us. I don't see that. Not too many prostitutes that I know do. We need all the help we can get. We'll support whatever we think is right, but don't mix other people's agendas up with ours.

MARIE ARRINGTON: The Alliance for the Safety of Prostitutes has alliances with Wages for Housework, but we are not a part of Wages for Housework. One of the things that the Alliance for the Safety of Prostitutes is demanding out of this whole society is that prostitution be a profession of choice and not one of necessity. We are not saying prostitution should not exist and that we want to abolish it. We are saying that we want prostitution to be for women that want to be in that profession, not because they have no other way to survive.

PARTICIPANT 2: I'm not a prostitute, nor am I in the sex trade. I'm wondering what I can do, and I feel sort of bound because I realize that I can't really liberate someone else. I can be sympathetic, but it's hard to know what sort of action to take. What Marie Arrington said about giving a nod of support — I think that's really important. But as far as fighting against Bill C-49 is concerned, what do you recommend? Is it my place to get a group of people together and demonstrate? I feel like I'm in a sensitive position, and I don't know what action I could take that isn't taking control of someone else or organizing around someone else's issues.

MARY JOHNSON: The first and foremost thing that every person can do is to write to Ottawa. Protest Bill C-49 *en masse*. For a little bit more militant strategy, if people are feeling really ambitious, we're going to find a lot of girls that are on the streets suddenly being arrested for communicating or attempting to communicate to people. If all women were out there standing with these girls, these women on the streets, it would be very hard for the authorities to ascertain which women were prostitutes. It would be very hard to ascertain who was in fact a communicating prostitute and who was a communicating person, if there should be such a distinction. It is fairly militant, but if people were willing to organize, things of this nature could be done.

CATHY: I have a friend who had a wonderful fantasy along those lines: we ladies should all go turn ourselves in at the jail and say, "Take me. I just communicated with this person on the street, and I know I'm chargeable. I confess, I confess." If we have five thousand ladies show up at West End Detention, they're going to have a problem.

PARTICIPANT 3: I'm a child care worker. I work with a lot of people who may at one point decide to change their circumstances. Sometimes for these kids the only way they get a decent night's sleep, three meals a day, and a warm home is when they're picked up. What percentage of jobs are blocked for people who have criminal records after they have been associated with prostitution or soliciting?

MARIE ARRINGTON: In Vancouver women who don't have criminal records have tried to get jobs, but the police have taken pictures of the women and have made them fill out cards, and they keep them on file. We have been taken inside the police station and shown these books. They have forced the women to stand in line on the street, taken their pictures, and filled out cards with their names and addresses. If they're transvestites, they include their street name, their sexual preferences, whether they use drugs, and what kind. All an employer has to do is phone the police station, give the name of the person trying to find a job, and they are already branded as a prostitute or a whore and not given that job. It's also much more difficult, once you've got a record, to break out of that.

I have asked where I work whether they knew women that wanted to quit the trade, and they have told me no. So I think it's next to impossible. Once you've been entrenched, it's very hard to break out — if you want to break out.

VALERIE SCOTT: With decriminalization we wouldn't have any criminal records. So if we chose to leave the business, that would be fine. We could do that. I'm not sure what exactly the percentage is right now with a criminal record. I've always been a whore, so I've never tried to get a straight job.

PARTICIPANT 4 (male): I've noticed that all the prostitutes have come out, but there's not a single person that has talked about going to a prostitute. This somehow has something to do with sex being bad. Well, I'll come out. I've been to female prostitutes, and I've been to gay hustlers. I've been in situations where people are not hustlers, but are somehow admitting that there is a means of exchanging sex for money. In Cuba a guy I was cruising came up to me and said, "Would you like to have a trio?" And I said, "Oh, my God. Well, my experience is that when somebody comes up to me in this situation, they want money, and in this particular case I'm not into it." He said, "What's the big deal? I want some running shoes, and you have money. I bet you earn at least $600 a month." What he wanted was a pair of shoes, and he was completely demystifying it.

Because "sex is bad," far too much importance is attached always to the financial transaction. What is bad for all of us is when it very clearly entails economic exploitation and forcing prostitutes to do something that they don't want to do. But there are many, many cases in which prostitutes are doing something that is valued and valuable to the customer or the client.

The marginalization of prostitution, the oppression of prostitution, is connected to taking sexuality out of much of the discourse on feminism and gay liberation. At a place like York University, to my knowledge, there is not a single course offered by somebody, for example, who is a lesbian, a transvestite, or a gay male in which their own sexuality is put on the table and openly acknowledged. So the people who are making fat incomes and have prestige out of talking and lecturing on these topics are accomplices in the marginalization, in the devaluation, of sexuality, which I think is connected to the oppression of prostitution — of prostitutes and sex trade workers.

MARY JOHNSON: With strippers and with prostitutes, I think the common general phrase is "those poor, exploited women that are being forced into doing something that they don't really want to do." Speaking as a dancer, that is not exactly true. We have chosen our professions for whatever reasons. I may not have decided when I was five years old that when I grew up, I wanted to be a stripper, but just the same, I did make a choice at one point.

If in fact we are those "poor, downtrodden women," it is because a prostitute can be evicted from her home for being a prostitute, because a dancer is arrested for doing her job, because our rights as human beings in this society are being taken away from us because of our chosen employment. It's not so much that we're being exploited by our trades or by the individuals that are in our trades, namely, the agents in the dancing industry or even the pimps in prostitution. We are free individuals that do have a choice. It is society that stops us at every turn — from having bank accounts, from acquiring loans, from seeking other employment, from using the knowledge and the street expertise that we have obtained in our professions as expertise or experience for any other line of work or any other way of life. That's where the *real* exploitation is.

CATHY: There is such a myth in this culture that the client is a sexual disfunctionate. He's a weird, perverted person with a trench coat, and he's strange, and nobody else will touch him. He's diseased like we are. You put together the whole gang of us — the pimp, the whore, and the trick — and the rest of the culture looks at these three entities and says, "My God. At the very best, we might do these people a favour and put them down in some warehouse district, in a red-light district. But for God's sake let's keep these misfits together because they all go together."

I would like to say that I like my clients. Some of my clients have been regular for seven years. I have people I see once a week or once a month. I have clients who, if I've been depressed myself, I've gone to see them, and I've sat there and cried and shared my story with them. This isn't to say that this is common practice, but it certainly does happen. I have clients that I care about. I think every prostitute, to a certain extent, has cared for some of her clients. They're not bad people. They're not evil people. So good for this man to stand up and say, "Yeah, yeah, sure, I've dealt with people. I've paid for sex." That's a very good thing for him to say because we can see that he's not a twisted and evil and distorted individual. It's nice; it's nice because the clients aren't like that.

If I'm sitting with a client down at the Harbour Castle hotel, and he's on his way from Sidney to Zurich to give lectures on banking, and he's sipping fine cognac, thank you very much, and we have a nice conversation and a reasonable sexual exchange, and I walk out of there with a fair amount of money, neither of us is quite as bad as some interests in the culture would like to have everybody believe.

I would also, on that same line of thought, defend the pimp — the infamous, terrible, horrible pimp, who's always Black, of course, always slick, just as women always have black eyes. Let's have some other, deeper, more sophisticated looks at that reality. I'm not condoning the men who do work several women, who are brutal — of course I'm not condoning that —but I would like to suggest to you that as adult women we have the right to choose our man, and we have the right to choose a good man, a bad man. I don't want the culture telling me what man I can live with. I don't like knowing that the police can come and take my man away at any moment. I could go home now and find him gone. The inferiority with which we are regarded is directed as well at the clients and the pimps and I suggest that it's not necessarily well founded.

PARTICIPANT 5: I thought that the attitude toward the running-shoes exchange sounded very trivializing. I think the attitude that he displayed toward openness and authenticity in the university system is demeaning and indicates that he hasn't even found out whether there are other people at universities in Canada who do lay themselves out by trying to put issues like this into the educational process.

VALERIE SCOTT: We're not talking about universities here. We're a bunch of whores.

PARTICIPANT 6: I'm a stripper, and I've also worked in theatre for several years. People talk a lot about the exploitation that sex trade workers experience, and they like to portray us as victims. In my experience as a stripper and as an actress it is a very unhappy thing for me to say that, unfortunately, I have felt far more exploited by some of my artistic colleagues and some of my so-called feminist sisters than I have ever felt as a stripper. I'm really sorry to have to say this.

PARTICIPANT 7: I just wanted to add to the statement about the customer. It is interesting that we, the prostitutes, are coming out first, and we're the most oppressed. The customers are still living in the shadows, and I'm wondering why they're last. I think it's because they belong. They are the property of other women, many of them. And therefore they are living in the harness of ownership of a woman. And maybe that's what we can start to look at. Most of them are married. And they're not going to come forward because they will jeopardize that marriage, because they will be seen as violating a sacred trust called marriage. Maybe we can start to look at this. Who are we really afraid of? Who are these men afraid of? What are women most afraid of? Are you afraid of losing property? I'm not talking to the feminists necessarily here. Is there maybe some part of you that has been having difficulty accepting prostitutes coming out because then you'd have to let your husbands come out?

PARTICIPANT 8: At certain points in a relationship that I may have with my man, we have agreements that we've come to. One of these may be that we will be monogamous. Whatever agreements you've come to is fine for you in that relationship. But I think the hard part is understanding when the rule or the agreement you've come to isn't the one that actually carries through. And many of us are wondering as women: is this actually happening to us and we are not aware of it? And maybe it's a question we should ask ourselves. I'm wondering — is it your experience that most men that you have as clients openly communicate this with their spouses or their partners?

VALERIE SCOTT: No, it's not openly communicated with the spouse. Most men that I see are about forty-five to fifty-five years old. The majority of them are married and have been married for twenty-five or thirty years. When you're with a person that long, sometimes — not in every case, but sometimes — you want a change. You may want to stay with your wife, you may want to still have the marriage with her. You may still be in love with her. But it doesn't mean that it's going to kill you to go out and have sex with a whore for an afternoon or an evening or an hour or thirty minutes. A lot of these men are still in love with their wives. Lust will never overcome love — ever. So let's not worry about it.

CATHY: We've all experienced lying in bed with a client in a hotel room, and he very casually phones Chicago and talks to his wife. "Hi, Sharon. How are you doing? How's Mikey, how's Johnny, how's Susie? Did Aunt Martha phone? Putting the kids to bed? Well, I'm just wrapping up my report now. I'm going get an early night. Okay, sweetheart. See you at noon tomorrow." And he's patting you on the leg while he's talking to his wife.

The man is truthful to a certain extent in saying that he is in love with his wife. She bears his children, she wears nice clothes, and his clothes are all the way from white to bright, and that's what the wife stands for. And she might have a garter belt and stockings for the odd little occasion, and he might allow her to indulge in a little bit of whorish conduct, but he knows deep down she's really a good woman, the mother of his children.

If his wife knew he had seen a prostitute, he'd be the first guy to say, "She didn't mean anything to me. That was just a little indiscretion, it was just a moment of pleasure. It was nothing. She's an object." What he's doing is dividing women, all women. He will not allow his wife to be sexual, and he will not allow the prostitute to be a creature of love and tenderness, and he's ripping them both off — badly.

I really try to not hate any particular figure in this panorama around prostitution. Everybody's a little bit guilty, and everybody's a little bit not so guilty. I often feel that our deepest enemies are the wives, the women who would like to believe that their husbands would not go to a prostitute. But no wife can ever be sure. She doesn't like us because she looks at us and wonders about that last trip he took to Miami. There's that little lingering doubt in there, and so she doesn't like us. It's a kind of a conspiracy in a way, isn't it? I don't know where it's going to go. I don't have any answers, but I know that the man splits women right down the middle.

PARTICIPANT 9: I'm a social worker. I run a street-based counselling service. I work with homeless and transient adolescents up to the age of twenty-one. My impression is that you are all in a more privileged position in terms of your working life as prostitutes than a lot of the women that I see. A lot of the women that I work with are trapped and are with bad pimps, and they get the same discrimination you all do by the cops and by other folks. I'd be interested in knowing at what point you make a distinction between child and adult. C-49 stinks, but I'm concerned about what happens — what protection you think there is for kids, particularly, who do get exploited on the street. Do you think there's legislation there now that is sufficient to protect adolescent women? If not, what would you suggest?

VALERIE SCOTT: I work on the street, and yes, there are a lot of kids out there. The young child prostitutes on the street haven't made a conscious decision to be prostitutes. They're there to survive. They're doing it to get money to get a place to sleep, some food to eat. They also do B and E's, they also rip off credit cards. They'll do anything they have to, to survive. Society continually whitewashes their problems with prostitution. I would like to see society look at these kids' problems, the whole issue — not just call them prostitutes and deal with them on that level.

As for when the distinction is made for becoming an adult, that's an interesting question. If your daughter or son showed tendencies toward ballet or piano, you would encourage them probably. Now if they showed tendencies toward prostitution, would you encourage them? My suggestion is, find out what the business is about and inform them. And if they choose to go that route, help them, because they'll do it anyway.

MARY JOHNSON: I also find it very interesting that they look at the child prostitute, and they say that the problem is prostitution. They forget about the problems of theft, drugs, or just general exploitation of youth on the street. Maybe the problems that started in their homes sent them there in the first place. You cannot look at the problems that our youth are having today and pin it on any one group. It's bordering on criminal for officials to try and say that prostitution is responsible for this.

Prostitution is a symptom of a greater problem that these children have experienced that put them on the street in the first place. Prosecuting prostitutes further and creating more legislation that will stop them from their rights as individuals in our society is not going to stop our problem of youth on the street. I can say for all of the ladies in the sex trade that we are just as concerned, if not more so, because we're exposed to it every day. We see these kids on the streets every day, and it breaks our hearts. But we are powerless to do anything about it, and we can only hope that society at large will address the problem where it starts. Parents must begin to understand what is happening with children today and why they are leaving their homes and what they are going to be exposed to when they do. A prostitute does not grab a child off the street and force her into prostitution. Other people do. The underworld does, the ruffian on the street, who will exploit anyone and anything, does. And that has to be acknowledged and dealt with.

MARIE ARRINGTON: There is a difference between what happens to kids on the street now and what happened when I was a runaway. Thirty years ago, when I ran, the women themselves on the street offered me alternatives so that I wouldn't have to turn a trick. So I survived in a multitude of other ways on the street. I did B and E's, I sold drugs, I boosted, I kept money for the women. I sat in a restaurant all night long, and the women would bring their money in; then at the end of the night they would give me a cut. When I have said this, I have been accused of pimping. It's not feasible nowadays to do those things; there are too many kids out there. Many women in Vancouver have taken kids down to emergency services and said, "Do something. This kid is strung out." But by the time the paperwork is done, the kid is out the back door, and nobody cares because these are society's disposable children. Kids can run for days, and the Badgley report is saying, "Punish them to forcibly treat them." The kids don't need treatment. They need money to survive, they need a good ear, they need a safe place to run to. None of these does society offer. So *we* have to do it. There has to be pressure put on by the people that pay the taxes to have these services offered.

CATHY: The young girls are a topic of constant conversation among my friends. At every public appearance I have made so far, the question is right there, as it should be: What do you do with the thirteen-year-olds, fourteen-year-olds? We feel that if we were decriminalized, if we were allowed to work in the same way somebody can work if they decide to open up a hardware store, we'd take care of our own kind, and we'd take care of them better than the culture itself has done so far.

We talk constantly about setting up hostels for these young girls, not letting them work, not letting them turn tricks. You bring them in, you give them food, you give them clothes. They don't eat much. Take care of them. But at the point we're at now, we aren't allowed to organize enough to even keep our own selves alive these days. We are not allowed to organize. Not being organized, we can't help the weaker members of our own community. We can barely help ourselves. Decriminalize us. Let us do some of that ourselves. We'll take care of the young girls. We would have houses for them, apartments for them. We'll bring them in.

PARTICIPANT 10: Cathy spoke about men who sip cognac and wear nice suits and call their wives in Chicago. Maybe it deserves to be very respectable, but I resent it when I hear people telling me that because a man wears a nice suit and sips expensive liqueurs, it's a more respectable act than maybe I would like to believe. I'm not saying it's disrespectful, I'm not making a judgment on you, but I don't like being swayed by fancy suits. Politicians wear fancy suits, and they do a lot of things that aren't good for people.

CATHY: Were you saying that I was giving him respectability because I described him as being affluent?

PARTICIPANT 10: I believe you were trying to create that impression, yes.

CATHY: We were discussing the clients' invisibility, the fact that no one knows who they are. I think that generally it is believed, and I think it's a belief of expediency for many interests, that the client is, sexually, a disfunctionate. I was just trying to say that the clients are not misfits particularly. You might run into the odd situation where there is somebody with a real problem. You deal with that, but by and large the clients are men. Look around you — the men in the room, clients.

PARTICIPANT 11: I was wondering if you could say something about the males in the sex trade.

MARIE ARRINGTON: There certainly are males out there in the sex trade. The boys get into it for the same reason: many of them running away from home need the money. Sometimes the boys are not accepted for their homosexuality and are kicked out of home and need the money. There are many boys hustling on the street that have girlfriends. Not all males working the street are homosexuals. But they do have a salability until they are a certain age, and once they hit that certain age and they're not cute enough or they don't have enough of a tight ass for the males that are driving around, then that's when they start cross-dressing. The whole myth is that the males are homosexuals and for homosexuals. Not true. It is the same men that are buying the girls that are buying the boys. And the younger they are, the more salable they are.

Males that are the hustlers that aren't cross-dressing don't experience the same kind of violence and to such a degree as the males who are cross-dressing. It's the transvestites that get the violence — not for being prostitutes, but for doing the horrible thing of cross-dressing as women. They are the ones that get chloroformed and hammered, and while they are being done in, it is always, "You fucking faggot! How dare you dress like a woman?!"

Still, it is much more acceptable in this society for a male to "sow his wild oats" and later get out of it and get into a job without being as stigmatized as women are.

PARTICIPANT 12: There is an assumption that it's always men seeking women or gay men seeking younger men. I have a copy of *NOW* magazine in my hands, and of course there are a lot of gay male hustlers who are advertising. But unless I'm mistaken, there are seven men who are advertising their services for women. Who are the women who are seeking male prostitutes, and what could be their reasons for doing so? There must be quite a large number of women who also want male prostitutes.

MARIE ARRINGTON: The women in this society just don't have the economic power to say, "I'm going to go out and spend $40 or $50 for whatever" because that means they're cutting into their budgets. And I don't think that at this point we've been socialized to go out and buy sex. That may be a while in coming, though I don't see it as an impossibility.

PARTICIPANT 13: I'd like to put in a plug for ambiguity and ambivalence because I would hope that the proceedings over the next couple of days will not degenerate into the kind of shouting matches that have taken place elsewhere in North America. I think there *are* things that can be discussed.

I find a lot of value in things that Margo St. James has said. But I guess I do stop at saying, as she apparently does, that the model that we should value the most right now for the ultimate goal of women's liberation is the model of the prostitute. I'm all in favour of equal pay for work of equal value, but I don't like the vision of a life spent servicing the sexual needs of heterosexual men.

MARGO ST. JAMES: Well, I don't think I'm holding up the whore as a model. I'm saying that the bottom line is, we're going to have to accept her choices if women are going to stop dividing each other.

PARTICIPANT 13: I agree. Let me just continue. I guess what I want to say is that I don't want to look to that as a model, but I want to take your approach as setting out a clear statement that we should move away from dichotomized modes of thinking, which I think would promote a state of valuing ambivalence.

PARTICIPANT 14: Margo St. James, how do you think the passing of the so-called Minneapolis Ordinance, the one "architected" by Catharine MacKinnon and Andrea Dworkin, would affect sex workers in the United States? I don't expect you to be familiar with the ins and outs of legislation here, but there are people who are looking at applying that to the Canadian situation, and I think it's important for us to understand its ramifications.

MARGO ST. JAMES: Well, I've been fighting with Kitty MacKinnon for a number of years, and I think the laws can be used against us. I'm against the censorship. To me pornography is an indication, an illustration, certainly not a cause, of the violence. The violence is there. It's everywhere — in our advertising, on our TV, especially in the States. So it worried me when I read the first draft of the bill, the one that was vetoed in Minneapolis. Two lines in that draft worried me and made me wonder where she was coming from. One line I objected to was "any look that invites penetration" — *period.* It didn't say with their own finger, with a dildo, by a cock, or what. So to me it looked like it was against any kind of heterosexual sex.

The other line that worried me tremendously was, "Pornography presents women as whores by nature." Well, what's wrong with that? I'm a bad girl. I like being a bad girl. I like my whore status. I have control and power over men, in private certainly, and now also in my public life. And I think men are afraid of the sexual superiority of women.

The Minneapolis Ordinance continues to divide women into good girls and bad girls. It is an interesting concept, however, that any group who is being maligned, whether it be Indians, Blacks, Jews, or anyone, should have the right, as you do in Canada, to prosecute anyone who incites violence against it. We should have something like that in the States, but we don't. Then we could tackle some of the problems of the violence on television and in advertising. It is not only pornography that has coupled violence with sexually explicit material.

PARTICIPANT 15: Margo St. James, you used the age twenty-one a couple of times. Is that the age at which you make a distinction between adults and children? Second, I'm not sure I understand why, as a woman, you would want your sexuality to be as much like a man's as possible, in terms of "fucking as many men as men fuck women." And third, how do you propose for hookers to be safe when women generally aren't safe in our society, when the people who make the legislation that exploits women on a variety of levels are also the people who are using hookers, who are also the people who are exploiting and harming women — whether they're on a street corner or with an escort service?

MARGO ST. JAMES: Okay, the age thing. We've had hookers' conventions for the last number of years, and we've had hot and heavy discussions about age. The medical reason for females not working commercially or having multiple partners is that before the age of twenty, if they have multiple partners, male partners, then they have a 30 percent higher chance of getting cervical cancer twenty years down the road. So it's a medical reason why we chose twenty-one. If we're going to do a mental thing, we'd choose twenty-five because we feel that a young person should find their own sexual self before they're subjected to a lot of commercial leering and lusting.

The right to fuck. I wasn't saying that I wanted to have my

sexuality like men's at all. I was saying that I want the right to have as many partners as I choose, and may they be whoever I want — men or women.

And as far as violence is concerned, I feel that the stigmatizing, the whore stigma, is what legitimizes violence, even in the home, because when the husband slugs his wife, he precedes the abuse with, "You slut!" "You whore!" So I think it's very clear that this official condemnation feeds the violence against women in general and that we have to stop it at the root, at the bottom line; otherwise, we're just putting bandages on it.

PARTICIPANT 16: I was getting offended by the antagonism toward feminism. And I don't think enough has been said about the fact that I'm a feminist, and I'm here and willing to listen, and I'm willing to work with prostitutes and try and reach a working middle ground. I understand the hurt you feel when women reject you because I've been rejected by liberal feminists who do not like my lesbianism. I don't think I should aim my hostility toward those women, but rather at what is behind that mentality, which is still "the man," which is still the patriarchy.

MARIE ARRINGTON: I was saying that I hope that what gets back to the women on the street is the support that is there. What is expressed within the feminist community is not said publicly enough and often enough. The papers only pick up the sensationalist garbage, and that's what the women get back. We want the feminists that are in support to speak louder and more often.

LESBIANS AND PROSTITUTES: A HISTORICAL SISTERHOOD

Joan Nestle

An expanded and revised version of this talk will appear in *A Restricted Country* by Joan Nestle, to be published by Nancy Bereano, Firebrand Books, 141 The Commons, Ithaca, New York, 14805.

Author's Note: The collage method used in this paper has certain dangers that I want my readers to be aware of. The first is that I am diluting the historical "specificness" of each instance of connection between lesbian *and* prostitute *because both of these terms have their own socially constructed legacies. Second, because I have culled the references from a wide variety of sources and I am in no way an expert in any historical period, I may be oversimplifying the resulting discoveries.*

However, I mean this work to be both factual and provocative, to break silences and to challenge assumptions, and most of all to provide the material for us all — the lesbian, the prostitute, and the feminist [who may be all three] — to have a more caring and complex understanding of each other so that we can forge deeper and stronger bonds in the battles to come.

I BEGAN WITH A QUOTE from a Manhattan community newspaper [dated June 17, 1985]: "Captain Jerome Piazza of the Manhattan South Public Morals Division estimates that there are at least 10,000 inside 'pros' in the city. Women Against Pornography contends that there are 25,000 prostitutes working inside and out within the city, over 9,500 of them on the West Side alone." When I saw this juxtaposition of a vice-squad policeman and Women Against Pornography giving statistics, I knew I had to do this work.

The original impulse behind this paper was to show how lesbians and prostitutes have always been connected, not just in the male imagination but also in their actual histories. Throughout I will use the word *whore*, and I will use the word *queer*; they're both used with love and self-claiming.

I hope that by putting out the bits and pieces of the shared territory of lesbians and prostitutes, I will have some impact on the contemporary feminist position on prostitution as expressed by the feminist anti-pornography campaign. However, while doing the reading and listening for this work, a larger vision formed in me. I developed the desire to give back to working women their own history, much as we have been trying to do in the grass-roots lesbian and gay history projects around the country. As I read about the complicated history of whores, I realized I was once again reading women's history, with all its contradictions of oppression and resistance, of sisterhood and betrayal. In my presentation I will try to honour both of these histories: those of the whore and the woman queer.

First my own starting point. In the bars of the late fifties and early sixties, where I learned my lesbian ways, working women were part of our world. We sat on bar stools next to each other, we partied together, and we made love together. The vice squad policed our world, and we knew that whore or queer made little difference when a raid was on. This shared territory broke apart, at least for me, when I entered the world of lesbian feminism. Whores and women who looked like whores became the enemy, or at least they were misguided, oppressed women who needed to be shown a better way.

Then in 1978, when I was reading through my mother's scribbled writings (which are her legacy to me), I discovered evidence that at different times in her life, my mother had turned tricks to pay her rent. I had known this all along, particularly the night I had shared her bed in the Hotel Dixie in the heart of 42nd Street, but I had never let the truth of my mother's life sink in. Then recently, in my own life, I have taken money for sex with women. And so it became clear to me, for both personal and political reasons, that this work on the shared history of lesbians and prostitutes had to be done.

The oldest specific reference to the connection between lesbians and prostitutes I found was in the early pages of William W. Sanger's *History of Prostitution*, published in 1859. As with reading historical references to lesbians, one must pry the women loose from the judgmental language they are embedded in. Prostitution, Sanger tells us, "stains the earliest mythological records." He works his way through the Old Testament, telling us that Tamar, daughter of Judah, covered her face with her veil, a sign of a harlot. Many of the women "driven to the highways for refuge, lived in booths and tents where they combined the trade of a pedlar with the calling of a harlot."

Two important themes emerge here: one of clothes as both an announcement and an expression of stigma and the other of women's work. It is in his chapter on ancient Greece that we find the first concrete reference to lesbian history. Attached to the Athenian houses of prostitution, called dicteria, "were schools where young women were initiated into the most disgusting practices by females who had themselves acquired them in the same manner."

A more developed connection is revealed in Sanger's discussion of one of the four classes of Greek prostitutes, known as the flute players. These gifted musicians were hired to play and dance at banquets, after which their sexual services could be bought. Once a year these women gathered to honour Venus and to celebrate their calling. No men were allowed to attend these rituals except with special dispensation.

Their banquet lasted from dark till dawn with wines, perfumes, delicate foods, songs and music. Once, a dispute broke out between two guests as to their respective beauty. A trial was demanded by the company and a long and graphic account is given of the exhibition [by the recording poet], but modern tastes will not allow us to transcribe the details.... It has been suggested that these festivals were originated by or gave rise to, those enormous aberrations of the Greek feminine mind, known to the ancients as lesbian love. There is grave reason to believe something of the kind. Indeed, Lucius affirms that while avarice prompted common pleasures, taste and feeling inclined the flute players towards their own sex. On such a repulsive theme it is unnecessary to enlarge.

My interpretation is somewhat different! The women sold themselves to men to earn a wage, but their love and pleasure they took in one another. The *lesbian continuum* that Adrienne Rich speaks about goes places we have not yet considered. One of them is the prostitute flute players pleasuring each other. This is perhaps the real roots of the Michigan Womyn's Music Festival, the yearly lesbian-feminist rite of music and physical freedom, including the rite to shed clothes and pleasure each other.

Throughout the history of prostitution runs the primacy of dress codes. This drama of how the prostitute has been socially marked in order to set her apart from the domesticated woman and what she did with these regulations is closely related to how lesbians have used clothes to announce themselves as a different kind of woman. Prostitutes, even up to the turn of the century, were described as unnatural women, creatures who had no connection to wives and mothers, much as lesbians, years later, were called a "third sex." In an 1830 text quoted in *The Lost Sisterhood: Prostitution in America 1900–1918* by Ruth Rosen, we are told that "she [the prostitute] could service men's needs because a great gulf separated her nature from that of other women. In the female character there is no midway. It must exist in spotless innocence or hopeless vice."

To ensure that prostitutes did not pass into the population of "true women," through the centuries states have set up regulations concerning her self-presentation and her movements. In Classical Greece all prostitutes had to wear flowered or striped robes. At some time, even though no law decreed it, working women all dyed their hair blonde in a communal gesture of difference. In the Roman period [Sanger writes] "the law prescribed with care the dress of prostitutes on the principle they were to be distinguishable in all things from honest women. Thus, they were not allowed to wear the chaste stola which concealed the form or the fillet with which Roman ladies bound their hair or to wear shoes or jewels or purple robes. These were the insignia of virtue. Prostitutes wore the toga like men, with their hair dyed yellow or red. Some even went one step further in a bold announcement of their trade and wore over the green toga a short white jacket, the badge of adultery."

For the next three hundred years prostitutes were marked by the state, both by being forced to wear a certain kind of clothes or markings, like a red shoulder knot, a white scarf and white ribbon, or yellow cords on their sleeves, and by being controlled as to where they could live and move about in cities. In medieval France they could only live in designated areas. They were forbidden to bare their heads and necks in public.

Yet within these controlled borders many of the women turned their social prisons into social freedom by becoming the intellectual free women of their day. Successful prostitution accomplished for some whores what passing as men did for some lesbians — it gave them freedom from the rigidly controlled women's sphere. "No women," [Sanger writes] "but the heteri [prostitutes] drove through the streets with uncovered faces and none but these mingled within the assemblage of great men."

Another source of information on the connection between lesbians and prostitutes is the autobiographies of great courtesans and madames. I will quote from an autobiography written in 1873 by Cora Pearl, who called herself "The Grand Horizontal." There is some question about the veracity of this version, but there is no doubt that she existed, and we hope that these are her words.

Her autobiography, entitled *The Erotic Memoirs of a Passionate Lady*, depicts a woman's life in the mid-nineteenth century. In it one discovers several lesbian worlds. The first is her world as a student in a French convent school for poor girls in 1849. Here the narrator discovers same-sex desires. "The degree of interest which my companions exhibited, not only in their own, but in each other's bodies was something strange to me." The author then goes on at length to describe a sexual initiation in a bathtub under the careful tutelage of Liana, an older student who brings both of the younger girls to orgasm as the rest of the girls watch. At night the courtesan-to-be says she "was taught the pleasures of the body, which within a year or two became so keen that I was convinced that anyone who neglected them was a dunce, indeed." It is also the language that fascinates me here — these pleasures were exclusively female. She carefully assures her readers, "These pleasures were never forced on any girl too young, too inexperienced to receive them."

She tells how she discovered that the older women, the school mistresses themselves, also enjoyed lesbian sex.

Suddenly going into one of the classrooms to fetch a set of needles, I discovered Bette on her knees before Soeur Rose, one of the younger and prettier mistresses, her head thrust beneath her skirts. I had time to glimpse an expression on her face which was familiar to me as that on the faces of my friends at certain times of mutual pleasure. Our nightly experiments in the dormitory can be imagined. Eugenie, my particular friend, hearing from Bette of the incident with Soeur Rose, determined to introduce me to the pleasure the lips and tongue can give, and I did not find that pleasure at all mitigated by distaste; then as since I was keenly conscious that one of the greatest joys of life is experiencing the pleasure that one can give to one's lovers. And now I was fully grown, and keen to experience myself the full extent of the pleasure I could give to others. For the most part, we fell into pairs and there grew up between many of us true and real devotion, unmatched since. On other occasions, when we were specially loving, three or four or five of us would come together to see what several partnerships of pleasure could be devised. And our experiments were by no means without their effect on my later career, for I learned at that time to be wary of no activity of which pleasure was the result.

Later on in her memoirs Cora relates the story of going to bed with the lesbian wife of a male client, a woman described in what I would call butch terms.

She then invited me to warm her, which being her guest I did. She was of a sturdy and muscular build, with breasts which were firm rather than full, indeed, no more presenting the chest of a woman than of some men I have known. . . . Not long after marriage she discovered that men and their figures were, if not entirely repugnant, at least unexciting to her, whereas admiration for the female figure was what she could not but give vent to. . . . Another woman must more securely know through pleasuring herself how to give pleasure to a fellow of her own sex.

In the world of women's history research we often hear the statement, "But women did not talk about sex in those days." And "those days" could be any century you choose. If we turn to the writing or the narratives of sexually defined women, however, like prostitutes, we may discover that there were women of different social positions who talked in all kinds of ways. The issue will be how we incorporate their lives into the *lesbian continuum*.

Another piece of evidence that testifies to the close, if not at times exchangeable, histories of lesbians and prostitutes is a sadder one. Mable Hampton, a Black lesbian woman who is now eighty-three and has been a lesbian her whole life, she says, was arrested in 1920 at a white woman's house. She was there waiting for her girlfriend. On some anonymous tip that a wild party was going on, three "bulls" [police] crashed through the door, and even though Miss Hampton was a "woman's woman," she was charged with prostitution and sent to Bedford Hills Reformatory for two years at the age of nineteen. According to Miss Hampton, many of the girls arrested for prostitution were lesbians. Mable summarizes her experience at Bedford by saying she "sure had a good time with all those girls."

This suggests that lesbianism and prostitution were seen as interchangeable crimes. We know from Ruth Rosen's book [*The Lost Sisterhood*] that from 1900 to 1918, the background period to Miss Hampton's arrest, prostitutes were the victims of anti-vice campaigns that established practices of harassment, surveillance, and arrest later to be used against clearly defined lesbians and their gathering places. "The growth of special courts, vice squads, social workers and prisons to deal with prostitution" became the lesbian legacy of the forties and fifties.

In *Prostitution in the United States* by H. B. Woolston a new technique for humiliating working women is clearly described. "A spectacular method of striking terror into the heart of the wrongdoers is the sudden and sometimes violent raid. A patrol wagon dashes up to the suspected house. Police scramble out and attack various entrances and exits and round up the inmates." Any lesbian who has been in a bar raid would recognize this description. Here is how a prostitute in the seventies describes a typical bar raid: "You can feel them in the air when you're in the bar and sometimes they take the whole bar out, all of the girls sitting in the bar and put them in the wagon, take them downtown and put them through a lot of hassles. They can just walk in and take you for I and D [idle and disorderly persons], if nothing else."

The prostitute, like the lesbian, has had to endure both medical and state intrusion into her life. One vivid example of how the two worlds come together is shown in an excerpt from an oral history by Rikki Streicher, owner of a lesbian bar in San Francisco. The time is the forties, but the incident has its roots in these anti-vice campaigns of the 1900s. The threat of disease was always the noose around the prostitutes' throats.

> I was working as a waitress at the Paper Doll. Somebody called out and said the cops were on the way. I sent everybody home and stayed, so I was the only one there so they took me in. If you were a woman, their charges were usually 72 VD, which meant they took you in for a VD test and 72 hours is how long they took for the test. They took me in, but decided not to book me, so a friend came down and got me out.

At the turn of the century the famous red-light districts of many American cities were born. I suggest that much undiscovered lesbian history lies in these so-called "dens of legalized vice": in New Orleans' Storyville, San Francisco's Barbary Coast, New York's Five Points and Tenderloin districts. [Rosen writes that] an ad in one of the famous blue books from this time, which was a directory of sexual services available in a district, similar to our *Gay Pride* guide, refers to female homosexual entertainment.

It is in "these segregated vice districts with their subcultures of developed language and folklore" that we can find some of the elusive lesbian working-class history we've been pining for. From this world comes the phrase "in the life" that will be used to designate a lesbian life, particularly by Black lesbians in the thirties and forties. From this world comes the use of a buzzer or light to signal the arrival of the police in the back room of a lesbian bar, a tradition still strong in the fifties. Rosen tells us that "these districts, although in a state of transition, offered women a certain amount of protection, support and human validation. The process of adapting to the life involved a series of introductions to the new language ... the humour and the folklore of the subculture." These words could also describe the experience of entering lesbian life in the pre-feminist fifties.

A prostitute in Kate Millet's *Prostitute Papers* will comment years later, "It's funny that the expression 'go straight' is the same expression for gay people. It's funny that both these worlds, the prostitute and gay world, should use that expression." The whole world that surrounded the working women at the turn of the century is echoed in the later bar and street lesbian culture.

In 1912 a lesbian prostitute anarchist named Almeda Sperry enters both histories by writing a love letter to Emma Goldman that uses a frankness of language we hunger for in our research.

> Dearest, it is a good thing that I came away when I did — in fact — I would have had to come anyway. If I had only had the courage enough to kill myself when you reached the climax then — then I would have known happiness, for at that moment I had complete possession of you ... Satisfied, ah God, no .... At this moment I am listening to the rhythm of the pulse coming in your throat. I am surging along with your lifeblood, coursing in the secret places of your body. I cannot escape the rhythmic spurt of your love juices.

Emma Goldman, we learn from Candace Falk's new work, *Love, Anarchy and Emma Goldman*, was no stranger to frank depictions of desire, so it comes as no surprise that she inspired such a passionate response. Almeda Sperry, lesbian and prostitute, should be as much a part of our history as Natalie Barney or the Ladies of Llanglollen. Neither her language nor her profession is genteel; she may not fit easily into academic reading lists. But the understanding of our history, of women's history, will be poorer for the exclusion of such voices.

In the forties in Howdy's, a New York open bar frequented by lesbians and featuring lesbian performers, I found out from an oral history that butch/fem prostitute couples worked the back tables with carefully laid-out plans of who would do what in terms of hand jobs and blow jobs. In doing the research for this presentation, I kept discovering clues to unexplored communities of both lesbians and whores. For example, according to the recollection of Dr. Virginia Livingston, the Brooklyn Hospital for Infectious Diseases had a clinic for prostitutes during World War II. Dr. Livingston said that many of the prostitutes were lesbians.

We have lots of evidence that not only did lesbians work as prostitutes but lesbians also visited prostitutes. Frank Caprio, a rather infamous pop psychologist of the fifties, tells us of brothels that were run for women and were referred to as "temples of Sappho": "Lesbian practices consist of intercourse via the use of a penis substitute, mutual masturbation, tribadism and cunnilingus. While many of the clients are passively homosexual, they often assume an active role and in this way they can find an outlet for their repressed homosexual cravings." In a 1957 work called *Cast the First Stone* we meet a young white woman who is introduced to both lesbianism and prostitution by Big Bertha, an older Black woman. Bertha is described as "not very pretty, only for a girl, but she would have been a swell-looking boy." She says, "Yeah, but should've been and was is two different matters, Tootsie Doll." The two meet in a training school for delinquent girls, and we are told that by the time the central character was ready to leave, she knew every trick of hustling that related to women customers as well as men. She had learned through Big Bertha and others that there were places in Harlem and elsewhere in New York where women came for thrills with other women.

In an interview in a 1972 women's paper, *Proud Women*, Maria Aldivito, a twenty-four-year-old lesbian prostitute, said she had been gay as far back as she could remember and a whore from age thirteen. She was also a passing woman. "Sometimes I went around passing as a man in straight places." (The role of butch women in prostitution also has an amazing and rich history, and it confounds all kinds of issues we think we know about.) Maria relates:

> Then I met a woman. We began doing things together, started living together. She took care of me, looked after me, introduced me to her tricks. When she left, I met some other chicks and ran them. I never took a cent of their money though. I loved them, they were my girls: I protected them. Chicks I ran with were all gay.

Asked why lesbians would be prostitutes, Maria said,

> Many of them can't get any other kind of jobs, especially dykes
> with short hair, and everybody knows they're gay and nobody's
> going to give them a job.

And then to bring us up to date, there is a little clipping from a
small paper called the *Tennessean*. In 1984 in a small town in
Tennessee the police set up an entrapment using policewomen as
prostitute decoys (decoys, by the way, were also used on lesbian
women in the fifties). After the arrests for soliciting were made,
the names of the arrested were published in the town's newspaper. In an article entitled "Police Sex Sting Nets 127," we hear
a woman's voice, one of the arrested would-be customers:

> "Some mistakes you can only make one time," said the only
> woman charged during the three-day undercover operation. "My
> mother and grandmother are ministers in Missouri; I'm not a low-
> life." The woman, who turned twenty-four today, sat in her car and
> wept after being given her citation. She was convinced she would
> be fired from her job, which she had only recently gained. "I do
> have some girlfriends, but things aren't great right now," she told
> the police decoy. She later told the reporter she thought the
> undercover operations were unfair. "I think the cop should have
> said, 'Hey, don't do it again' and let me live my life. You're talking
> about a story. I'm talking about my life."

Finally, I've been doing interviews with working women. Katie
is a gay civil rights activist, a worker for New York Women
Against Rape, and a labour organizer. For three years she worked
in a Madison, Wisconsin, brothel at night while she waitressed in a
lesbian greasy spoon called Spudnik's during the day. She said, "I
looked like a gym teacher gone astray. My house name was Sam."
(As soon as she told me this, I thought of the bars in the fifties
where many women had a bar name — another echo.) She said,
"It was one of the best jobs I had because I made a lot of money,
had the most control, and was part of the community that I still

call on." She's quick to point out that this is not true for all working women. She says that turning tricks helped demystify men and that her lover at the time, an older butch woman, never gave her a hard time because of her work.

Katie brings the two worlds into the eighties. She has developed a feminist analysis of class and gender ("inseparable," she says) and a deep understanding of how all women run in fear of these two words: *whore* and *queer*. "One woman alone," she says, "is a whore. Two women are lesbians. Control over women from the fear of these two accusations is encoded in the law."

Lesbian prostitutes have suffered the totality of their two histories as deviant women. They have heard the church, the doctors, and the state call them sinful, sick, unnatural, and a social pollution. In many ways the history of prostitution or of the prostitute is also the history of the lesbian. Lesbians and prostitutes created and lived in a subculture that gave evidence to their oppression and their resistance. Language and dress were both used to reveal stigma and to break its hold.

In the eyes of the outsider, particularly in the psychological world, there never was any question about the connection between lesbians and whores. Both lesbians and prostitutes were and are concerned with creating power and autonomy for themselves in seemingly powerless social interactions. In the words of a lesbian prostitute, "I'll make sure I'm out of there in ten or fifteen minutes. I'm always keeping my eye on the time, and *I* decide how long I'll stay, depending on the amount of money and what the guy is like. I never stay longer than an hour unless the money makes it worthwhile. They want more, but in the end we set the terms of the relationship, and the Johns have to accept it." Another woman goes on to say, "From the point of view of the working girl, control and power must always be in our hands if we're to survive."

The class structure that exists for prostitutes also exists for lesbians. The closer to the street you are, the more deviant you are seen to be. Call girls and professional lesbian women have things in common. They both have more protection, more acceptance than the streetwalker or the bar dyke, but coming out to the wrong people can deliver them both into the hands of the state. Both are often in a hurry to disconnect themselves from their sisters in the street in an effort to lighten their own feelings of difference.

I think that one of the ironies at this time is that we as lesbians have more legal and communal power than prostitutes do. A spokeswoman for Pony Prostitutes of New York said in 1980, "If the hookers and the housewives and the homosexuals got together, we could move the world." But in order to do this, we must face the challenge of our own histories, the challenge of understanding how the lesbian world stretches from the flute players of Greece to the Michigan festival of lesbian separatists.

Why has this seemingly obvious connection between these two groups of women gone so unspoken in our current communities? What impact has cultural feminism and classism had on this current silence? Will a reunion of these two histories, which in many cases are one, give us a stronger political grasp of how to protect both prostitutes and lesbians in these fearful times? If we can make any part of the world safer for these two groups of women, we will make the world safer for all women because "whore" and "queer" are the two accusations that symbolize lost womanhood, and a lost woman is open to direct control by the state. Call me whore or call me queer — I am a working woman who loves women, and I have a right to do it in safety and dignity under my own control and on my own terms. The earliest Biblical descriptions of the prostitute say that she is brazen, full of arrogance and rebellion. In the Book of Proverbs we are told she is "loud and stubborn and her feet abide not in her house." I know this woman, for she is part of us.

BIBLIOGRAPHY

Caprio, Frank. *Female Homosexuality: A Psychodynamic Study of Lesbianism*. New York: Grove Press, 1954.

Falk, Candace. *Love, Anarchy and Emma Goldman*. New York: Holt, Rinehart and Winston, 1984.

Hampton, Mabel. Tapes in possession of Lesbian Herstory Archives, New York City.

Maria. "Maria: A Prostitute Who Loves Women." *Proud Woman* 11 (March–April 1972): 4.

Millet, Kate. *The Prostitution Papers*. St. Alban's, N.Y.: Paladin Books, 1975.

Otis, Leah Lydia. *Prostitution in Medieval Society*. Chicago: University of Chicago Press, 1985.

Pearl, Cora. *The Erotic Memoirs of a Passionate Lady*. New York: Stein and Day, 1983. First published in English, 1890.

"Police Sting Nets 127." The *Tennessean*, November 22, 1984. Rosen, Ruth. *The Lost Sisterhood: Prostitution in America 1900–1918*. Baltimore: John Hopkins University Press, 1982.

Sanger, William. *History of Prostitution: Its Extent, Causes and Effect Throughout the World*, New York, 1876.

Streicher, Rikki. Excerpt from interview that appeared in *In the Life* 1 (Fall 1982). Publication of the West Coast Lesbian Collection (available at the Lesbian Herstory Archives, New York City).

Tayler, Katie. From an interview conducted in spring 1986.

Turrill, Barbara. "Thirty Minutes in the Life." Transcript of a talk for WGBH radio, May 13, 1976. Available at Lesbian Herstory Archives, New York City.

Woolston, H. B. *Prostitution in the United States Prior to the Entrance of the United States into the World War*. 1921. Reprinted, Montclair, New Jersey: Patterson-Smith, 1969.

WATCHING MYSELF
ON STAGE

Petal Rose

I WAS AFRAID TO attend this conference on pornography and prostitution, let alone speak or perform at this political event. There was talk of cameras from the media. Masks were considered to be strictly for chicken-shits, inappropriate for women who should be, in this day and age, coming out of their "closets of shame." Working girls, those who have gone bare-assed for so long, should now be going bare-faced, like Val Scott and Peggy Miller. Whores today, like the suffragettes of yore, should be going public all the way.

Well, I thought, that philosophy is great for women who dabble in whoredom or who have masochistic tendencies, but for me going public is scary. I work all day and all night in the sexual arts trade; however, my work is not legal in Canada. I'm no Joan of Arc. I'd rather wear feathers than armour.

So I didn't give a workshop, and I didn't participate as a curious member of the public. But when my good friend Janet Feindel called and said she was going to perform a theatre piece based on my life — I had to go. After all, I'm my own biggest fan.

Various acts were scheduled to perform that evening. I sat in eager anticipation with a friend, Gwendolyn, who is also a performer. Early in the program we were presented with slides of female genitals. My mind flashed back to the early seventies in Detroit, where I went with my dancing partner to what was then considered to be a hard-core porn movie house. That was the first time I saw large blow-ups of female genitals.

Even before her show I began to admire my friend Janet. She has to have guts to get up in this hall full of outspoken feminists. I'm glad she's going up there as an actress/playwright doing me instead of me going up there doing me. This way we're both safe.

Then Janet comes dancing down the aisle, all painted up and tarted out in flashy trash. I wince. Her face is painted like a clown, and she's wearing a shiny purple jersey. And she's handing out treats. She's skipping like a happy-go-lucky child. Is this how Janet sees me? As a self-appointed critic of the show, I don't think this persona is particularly appealing. I make a mental note to have a chat with Janet about some possible changes in the visual effects.

Then Janet starts to speak. She is using funny speech mannerisms. She is lisping and pinching her lips together and verbally crossing her t's. "Oh, my God, is that how I sound?" I ask Gwendolyn. She nods. I'll have to have a chat with myself about some speech improvements. I'm going to start working with a tape recorder right away. "My" speech habits, as I hear Janet continue, seem irritating, contrasting with the important things "I" have to say.

This is the first time I have seen Janet display her talents with her clothes on. Up until now I've only seen her perform as a stripper. Apart from her makeup and costume, I am very impressed with her performance. Her acting ability is good. She looks beautiful, highly animated, and in perfect physical shape. I wonder how she keeps so fit, as she only strips part-time between her acting jobs. Her gestures are spontaneous, subtle, and appropriate. Her lines are delivered with expert timing.

I start to relax and listen to what she has to say as Petal Rose. I am amazed at her memory. I wonder if she was carrying a small tape recorder in her purse during our past conversations. She picks out stuff I have long forgotten. It all sounds great up on stage. I start to laugh. Other people are laughing too. To my ears everything sounds kind of odd and warped, but most of all true.

They say imitation is the highest form of flattery. I love every minute of it. Mirrors, even the fun house ones that can make one appear distorted, have always turned me on.

PART THREE

SEX TRADE WORKERS AND FEMINISTS SPEAK

PART THREE OPENS BY dealing with the issue of racism and organizing, which became a major concern to participants and conference organizers. Some of the background is discussed in the Introduction. This section includes statements from Lesbians of Colour, from the Racism in Pornography workshop participants, and from me on behalf of the Conference Organizing Committee.

The final panel of the conference posed the question, Pornography: What Do We Want? Varda Burstyn, one of the panelists, suggested that a more fundamental question needed to be posed first, that is, "Who the hell is 'we' anyway?"

Part Three deals not so much with the first question as with the underlying questions of who is a good girl, who is a bad girl, and who decides who's who.

The pieces by Susan G. Cole, Varda Burstyn, Marie Arrington, and Valerie Scott were all presentations made during panel sessions. The remarks by Amber Cooke and the Canadian Organization for the Rights of Prostitutes are excerpts from interviews conducted after the conference and are based on their workshop presentations.

From the Closing Session: On Racism and Organizing

LAURIE BELL (A CONFERENCE ORGANIZER): Because of what is happening here in our own city and in our own country right now, the focus of this conference has been on Canada. Consequently, we have not sufficiently addressed what is happening with pornography and prostitution in the world, especially in developing nations. We'd like to acknowledge the lack of a global perspective.

Another omission that we must acknowledge is the analysis that links prostitution with militarism; that analysis was not represented fully this weekend.

PARTICIPANT 1: Could I interject here please? I have a statement to make from the Racism in Pornography workshop. I think while you're talking about omissions, it's really good to put it in right here. You're talking about focusing here on the home front and forgetting about brothers and sisters around the world. Well, I think you forgot about the brothers and sisters right here as well.

I have two criticisms from the workshop. One of them is the lack of Women of Colour in the forums and workshops. The other is the lack of analysis of racism as a central component of pornography and prostitution by the women who did speak at the forums and workshops.

Our two basic recommendations are: first, a conference challenging our images is incomplete without explicitly incorporating an anti-racist perspective throughout the program; and second, women with privilege and influence must use their positions and resources to challenge racism in the sex trade and in society. This is something we should think about while we're talking about omissions.

PARTICIPANT 2: I have a statement from Lesbians of Colour. We present this statement in solidarity with our Native sisters. We were angry and appalled at the racism and racist imagery in one of the performances last night and the audience's complicity with it. Native women were attacked by the performer, and most of the audience showed their blatant acceptance of racism by applauding. However, it is important to remember that a small number of the people in the audience challenged this performer's racism. What happened yesterday is just one of the ways in which racism has been a central aspect of this conference. It indicates to us that there remains a lot of work yet to be done. We must all find ways of recognizing and challenging racism wherever it occurs, whenever it occurs — which is all the time. We demand a public apology to Native women from the performer and accountability by the organizing committee for racism expressed in this performance.

LAURIE: Thank you. After we ask the question, "What has been missing?" we have to ask the question, "And what has happened?" One of the things that has happened this weekend is that during last night's performance blatant racist remarks were made during one of the performances. These remarks are neither condoned nor acceptable to the organizing committee. However, we should not let the blatancy of that racism and that racist blunder divert us from acknowledging the many, many layers of racism and classism and many other "isms" that have been operating this weekend on the part of not only sex trade workers and performers but also feminists and all people who have been participating in and organizing this event.

If some of us don't make blatant racist blunders in public, it is not because we are not racist, but because we are becoming aware enough of our racism to avoid doing that in public. I want to read something to you. This is written by Bernice Johnson-Regan, who is a member of the a cappella singing group Sweet Honey In The Rock. This is an excerpt from "Coalition Politics: Turning the Century" published in *Home Girls: A Black Feminist Anthology*.

> When it comes to political organizing and when it comes to your basic survival, there are a few people who took the sweep from the 60's to the 80's and they didn't miss a step. They could stand it all. If they're painters, there's a picture about everything as best they can do. And if they're singers, there's a song showing that they were awake through all the struggles. Now the songs and the pictures and poems and performances ain't all right, 'cause you ain't dealing with people who are free from bigotry. I remember a song I wrote about Vietnam. It wasn't about Vietnam, it was about the whole world. And it started, of course, with Black people — I don't start nothing except with Black people.... [One verse was:] "The Vietnamese, with slanted eyes, fighting for their land, not standing by. They can't make it 'cause there's no room." Okay, did you see what I did? Reduced these people to the slant of their eyes. If I ran into a Vietnamese who didn't have slanted eyes, I'd be in trouble. They may not have even had slanted eyes, but you know when people talked about them, they had slanted eyes.... Do you understand what I'm talking about? So all of these people who hit every issue and did not get it right, but if they took a stand, at least you know where their shit is.

So some of the shit's on the floor, and somehow all of us are going to go on from here. Our intention for this conference was to attempt to better our understanding and learn to improve the dialogue between each other — not only between sex trade workers and feminists but also between men and women and between various points of view within the feminist community and within the sex trade industries. And we acknowledge that we must keep the dialogue going on many, many of these fronts.

PORNOGRAPHY: WHAT DO WE WANT?

Susan G. Cole

THE TITLE OF THIS CONFERENCE is Challenging Our Images. My perspective on pornography, I have discovered, is not only challenging to those people who think everything is just fine but also challenging in a way to the original feminist perspective that was offered in the early stages of our protest against pornography. I have found that my perspective has been questioned by pro-pornography as well as anti-pornography feminists and non-feminists.

I first got interested in the issue of pornography about eight years ago, when a movie called *Snuff* came to Toronto. *Snuff* was advertised by its producers as featuring the actual murder of a prostitute from "South America, where life is cheap." The actual murder of this woman was advertised as a sexual turn-on. When I discovered *Snuff*, I thought it was a bit much.

And so we began, myself and other feminists, to look at pornography and see what's really there. We saw women being brutalized, we saw women being tied up, we saw women being tortured, we saw women being maimed. We came up with a very convenient formulation so that we would be totally pro-sex: it wasn't the sex, it was the violence that upset us. Leaving aside that the violence was there to turn people on sexually and that therefore sex was at least somewhat implicated, my subsequent explorations have revealed that this formulation is not quite enough. In other words I'm not entirely convinced that looking for degradation is going to really solve our problems of understanding what pornography is and does.

I learned a lot about what pornography is and does by reading a book called *Ordeal*. It is about Linda Marciano, who at the time was Linda Lovelace and who was the star of the single most commercially successful pornographic film ever made, called *Deep Throat*. It is about a woman with a clitoris in her throat. This film was made while Linda Lovelace was being pushed around and brutalized by her pimp and by the makers of this film. The problem is that if you look at the film, you don't see the brutalization on the screen. What you see is all of that groovy consensual sex that everybody wants to see represented and that everybody thinks is just fine. This is why my work is in this area and why I'm thinking of entitling my work about pornography *This Book Is Not Just about Pictures*. We have to stop only looking at the pictures to figure out if pornography is happening.

After I began to listen to Linda Marciano, I decided that it was much more useful for feminists to look at the whole production, the whole package — to look at how pornography is made, to look at the pictures, to understand that it's there for sexual pleasure or gratification — and also to begin to look at the conditions of the people, mostly women, who are in the product available to consumers. Consequently I define pornography not as pictures, but as a practice. To understand the concept, think about photography. A photographer sets up a chemical change to get the picture, and then you have the photograph. But photography is the whole package. An advertiser does things in order to give you a picture so that you will go and buy a product. I urge you, when you think about this issue, to stop looking only at the pictures because you won't get all your answers there.

Women and feminists have known that it's much more important to look at our own experience and the experience of real people. We've seen the façade of a perfectly happy marriage and known that maybe something else was actually going on there. Although it is not always the case, often the women are coerced and forced into performing for pornography. This I refer to as *sexual subordination*. My definition of pornography is the practice of presenting sexual subordination for sexual gratification. That's how I see it. This is a tool for analysis to figure out whether pornography is happening.

I want to unpack some of the aspects of this practice. First the conditions under which these things are made. I noticed, for example, that the pictures really weren't going to tell the whole story because people had been looking at pictures of women being brutalized and not noticing that there might be some harm there. Instead we have judges saying, "One man's this is another man's that." Or our own customs agent, who, when asked how he didn't notice that *Penthouse* in December of 1984 was distributing photographs of women being tightly bound, hanging from trees and pegs and rocks, said, "Well, the violence is only implied."

I realized that the pictures aren't going to help us because pornography has been so successful that we're not even real people anymore — we're only things. People don't even notice that anything's going on in the material where a woman is being harmed, let alone where there is the appearance of consensual sex going on. Women are being brutalized whether the gun is in the camera frame or not.

Next, looking at the picture, I note that it is there to turn somebody on. The pictures are supposed to be doing something. This is not a fantasy. Neither is it an idea. This may not apply to the lesbians in the room, but the next time any of you apprehend an erection, either your own or somebody else's, look at it very carefully and tell me that it's a fantasy. Tell me it's an idea, and if it is speech, what is it saying?

Now I want to address the issues surrounding the consumption of this material. I could sit and quote you clinical studies from all kinds of people who have been doing work in laboratory settings, but I will not. Some of this work is valuable because it's being done by men, and so people believe them. But I don't need some man to sit in a laboratory and tell me that rape is happening.

I've been talking to women and asking them what they think about pornography and what pornography has meant in their lives. I have been talking to a particular group of women, admittedly — I have been surveying shelters for assaulted women. I ask, "What does the word *pornography* mean to you?" They talk about being terrorized. They talk about men saying, "Look at that. Why can't you do that? Replicate that." The men don't know that Linda Lovelace did that because she was forced to do it and not every woman wants to do it. When these women tell me what is happening to them, I believe them. And if we don't believe them, nobody else will.

Sometimes the pictures are pretty clear about what they are doing to sexuality. They are making sexuality look pretty much one-dimensional, that is, men on top, women on the bottom — period. You see the hierarchy, the violence, and the definition of *male* fused with dominance and the definition of *female* fused with submission. They are making inequality sexy. Not only are they making inequality sexy, they are making it sexual.

Consider how difficult it has been to reverse the situation. Bob Guccioni and the *Penthouse* empire tried to sell beefcake to women the way he sold cheesecake to men. He produced a magazine called *Viva* in 1972. It featured sexually explicit accounts of women's sexual adventures punctuated with male nudes. The problem was where to display it. Put it beside *Playboy* and *Penthouse*, and he doesn't get his targetted audience. Put it beside *Chatelaine* and *Good Housekeeping*, and he causes apoplexy among the readers of those magazines.

But eventually he did find his audience. Women were delighted.

They used to have to settle for *Cosmopolitan* telling them how to land Mr. Right. Now they found out what happened once he was in hand, and they liked it. But they started to complain. They said, "These guys look gay." The producers of *Penthouse* did everything they could to make sure that this would not happen. They knew that if you spread a woman's legs and put her looking at a camera, she'll look sexy. But you can't do it with men. So they tried everything. They had him in forest settings. They had him looking out into the distance to make him look like he had control over the whole environment. They had him on horses so that he could look like the Marlboro man. And they still looked gay. This is not to cast aspersions on my gay brothers, but rather to say that when women looked at these pictures, they did not see what they considered masculine by conventional standards. My point is that if you reduce a woman to tits and ass, she'll look like a woman, but reduce a man, and he will not look masculine according to our standards.

When sexual abuse is eroticized and distributed to the tune of $8 billion dollars a year on this continent, with more outlets than there are McDonald's, this makes women feel like we're second-class citizens. We wonder: if this goes on as entertainment, how are we being viewed in society? The fact that people can look at the pictures and not see women getting hurt is even more of a problem.

Racism is being sexualized just as inequality is being sexualized. The image of Black women in pornography is almost consistently one featuring them breaking from chains. The image of Asian women in pornography is almost consistently one of being tortured. The best way to institutionalize a dynamic of power is to eroticize it.

Obscenity laws are a problem for us, and I think we have to oppose them. Obscenity laws do two things. First of all, they rely on community standards, which in a sexist and heterosexist society are bound to be sexist and homophobic. It's no wonder that so much gay material comes under fire. My problem with community standards is that they suggest, as Catharine MacKinnon has said, that the problem with the pornographer is that he has chosen the wrong audience. If he could only find one that put up with women being hung up on meat hooks, everything would be just fine. My main problem with obscenity laws, though, is that they look only at the pictures. In Winnipeg Judge Ferg, looking at sexually explicit pornography, looked at a movie and said, "I see consentual sex here. This is not obscene." I'm sure there are some people in this room who think that this was a great breakthrough for sexually explicit material — because he looked at consensual sex, and he said it was not obscene. Guess which movie he was looking at? *Deep Throat*! You see the problem.

The question is, what do we want? Here's what I want. I want a legal remedy that will give relief to women who are harmed by the practice of pornography. I want a legal remedy that's going to stop looking at the pictures, stop calling them fantasy, stop calling them representations and images and depictions and start viewing them as documents, presentations, and the reality of women and men in this culture. If men look carefully enough at the pictures, they may notice that pornography makes male sexuality look like that of a rapist, and they should be upset about it. I want a legal remedy that's going to redress harms. This is why I'm sympathetic to the Minneapolis Ordinance approach, which defines pornography as a violation of women's civil rights. When men look at pornography, they see tits and ass. That's all. That isn't to say that our sex is bad, but we are more than that. It's important to expand the issue from "Oh, it's just about sexuality" and understand how all of this is affecting all of our lives everywhere.

I would really like to see as much time as is spent eroticizing inequality and hierarchy and dominance and power and violence and brutality spent on eroticizing equality. I don't even think we know what it would look like! And my greatest fear is that if we looked at it, we wouldn't even be turned on by it anymore.

WHO THE HELL IS "WE?"

Varda Burstyn

THE PARTICIPATION OF ARTICULATE sex workers has marked a new stage in the discussion of issues of sex and politics among feminists in this province, if not in this country. Also, by the tenor of the discussions at this conference, it seems to me that we are maturing, and in the process changing the idea of what we mean when we say "we."

When asked the question, Pornography: What Do We Want? [the title of this panel], I had trouble answering because, as I realized when I thought about it, it begged another question, namely, who the hell is "we" anyway? To ask what "we" want implies that there's a homogeneous consensus on how we approach sexuality, sexual representation, and sex work. It certainly does not exist with respect to that large and various discourse we call, all inclusively, pornography. There isn't that kind of unanimity. For a long time there hasn't been that kind of unanimity among feminists even with respect to prostitution. The consensus that might have appeared before or that operated as a kind of "public face" feminism is crumbling in a very healthy way. We are all learning that if we're going to have a "we" that really works for feminists and for feminist supporters, it has to be more inclusive.

Susan Cole has given a succinct, intelligent, and witty summation of the sort of major line of feminist criticism of pornography that has been developed by her, by Catharine MacKinnon, and by Andrea Dworkin over the last few years. This represents one important strand of feminist thinking. But feminist voices that propose different approaches with respect to both the interpretation of pornography and strategies to "deal" with it have also been raised.

My impression from travelling and speaking is that the growth of these voices has put the automatic use of the term "we" into question in a healthy way. These voices, which don't deny a number of the points that Susan made about some aspects of pornography, do stress, however, that pornography — in the sense of sexually explicit material created for the purpose of arousal — is not only or exclusively a discourse of misogyny and violence against women nor always experienced as that by women or men. The growing articulation of this view, and the associated rejection of the censorship strategies, come just in time. At least I hope it's in time and not too late.

Sheila Noonan outlined some decisions by the courts that she saw as positive, decisions that looked at various pornographic texts and said, for example, "Consensual gay sex is part of the community standard of tolerance, so it's all right. Explicit sex is fine. But violence is not. Various other kinds of fetishes and so-called perversions are not all right." She interpreted those decisions as positive because they reflected a feminist concern about sexism and violence rather than a puritanical pre-occupation with keeping sex hidden. She interpreted those decisions as a sign that the "feminist critique" is becoming more generally understood, that it's actually reaching that rather encrusted layer of men who sit on the bench and pass judgment on many aspects of our lives. I wish I could say that these decisions represent the majority tendency in the judiciary and in society, one that points to a firm, clear direction. But I think there's something else at work, a stronger tendency in the political culture — and a reactionary and frightening one.

We have spent a lot of time talking about Bill C-49. Bill C-49 did not drop from the skies, and it is not alone on the sexual-political landscape as a troubling phenomenon. A number of recent legal decisions and government actions are consistent with the spirit of this bill. In September 1985 the Supreme Court of Canada decided that the issue of community standards had to be judged as a measure of average Canadian tolerance. In other words, what may take place in an arts bookstore on Queen Street in Toronto must be judged according to the same standards that apply in Goose Bay, Newfoundland.

In effect you can't win with the community standards approach because, as Susan has pointed out, in a homophobic, heterosexist society community standards are bound to reflect anti-gay and anti-woman values. Nevertheless, we now face a decision that effectively reduces those standards to the lowest common denominator, and we know how conservatizing this can be when it's filtered through the social-control apparatuses: the government bureaucracies, the law enforcement agencies, and the judiciary.

Another troubling Supreme Court decision dealt with genitally shaped sex toys. In the grand scheme of things, whether there are more or less penis-shaped dildos manufactured means nothing to me. But two things about the decision to ban them *do* mean a great deal. First, sex toys — especially vibrators and dildos — have nothing to do with violence, brutality, or sexism, and the decision to outlaw them has nothing to do with an anti-violence, anti-coercion feminist agenda. But this decision took advantage of the climate of fear and shame surrounding sexual commodities that has been created by feminist campaigns.

Second, the Supreme Court decided to rule on these objects even though they were not covered by the obscenity clauses in the Criminal Code. The court dubbed them "publications" that "unduly exploited sex." This may be absurd, but it is not a light matter. The court had a choice. It could have declined to rule on this matter — after all, who do these objects harm? — or it could have ruled in favour of the defence. Instead it expanded the law in a frightening fashion — what else can be dubbed a publication for the purpose of banning? — in a classically sex-repressive decision. The choice is an important indicator of the general political climate and of a different thrust, if I may use that term, to the one Sheila Noonan has noted in the judiciary.

The next point is even more worrying. The rate of confiscation of gay and lesbian material is now at an all-time high. Even William French, writing in the quietly and respectably homophobic *Globe and Mail*, expressed alarm about this development. The legislation under which the confiscations are being conducted was put into place as an emergency measure following the feminist outcry over the photo spread of bound Japanese women in the December 1984 issue of *Penthouse* magazine. Again feminists' concern about violence against women is being used to implement an anti-gay agenda.

The Joy of Gay Sex has been removed from bookstore shelves, although *The Joy of* (heterosexual) *Sex*, including its section on bondage and S/M, remains untouched. *The Joy of Lesbian Sex* is also being seized. [As this book goes to press, the anti-gay confiscations have become so large and inclusive — books by Tennessee Williams, Allen Ginsberg, Radclyffe Hall, and many others have been seized — that they've put the continued availability of gay and lesbian erotica, as well as the financial viability of several gay and lesbian bookstores, into question. The seizures are being contested under the Charter of Rights, but the cases may take several years to resolve. In the meantime the confiscations proceed. — Editor]

Finally we have the Pages bookstore case. Pages is a bookstore on Toronto's Queen Street, one of the most important bookstores in the Toronto arts community. Last May, in the context of a feminist arts festival, the management asked three feminist artists to set up their installation "It's A Girl" — a kind of found-object collage of over 150 items that reflect different aspects of women's lives — as a backdrop to its feminist book display. (The display included Andrea Dworkin's and Susan Griffin's well-known anti-pornography books.) Among these items were some paint-splattered menstrual pads and tampons and, along the bottom of the display, some plaster phalluses representing men and masculinity. Judy Chicago and her students created " The Menstrual Bathroom" in their "Women's House" in Los Angeles in the early seventies, and issues of menstruation have been an important theme in feminist art since then. This did not stop the police from charging the bookstore with obscenity and arresting its manager.

Despite petitions to him from prominent members of the arts community, Attorney General Ian Scott has refused to drop the charges, forcing Pages and the arts community to mount an expensive, time-consuming case, thereby ensuring that regard-less of the verdict the chill of censorship will be felt. [After one and a half years Judge Harris ruled in favour of the defence and suggested that the "disgusting object" clause under which the prosecution was conducted had no legitimate place in Canadian law. The wording of the proposed new pornography legislation, which would criminalize depictions of menstruation and lactation, should it be passed into law, will effectively nullify Judge Harris' intent. — Editor] The artists, a group called the Woomers, are feminist artists, and they didn't have any imagery pictures that could possibly be co-opted by the patriarchy. Their display was witty, snarky, sarcastic. It was a kind of joke, but it was not a kind of porn. The police did not get the joke.

Why am I so worried about this? Because it seems that feminist concerns about violence are being used as a cover for an anti-feminist agenda on sexual representation. This is not something we like to think about because it's frightening to realize that such important components of the institutions that govern in our name can be so much against us. But we have to face the facts. It's clear from Bill C-49 that Justice Minister John Crosbie couldn't care less about feminist concerns over sex work. Nor does he care much about feminist concerns over women's sexual objectification. As Susan Cole often points out, he's the guy who brought Shannon Tweed, *Playboy* Playmate of the Year, to appear at a fund-raising gala for him. *Playboy* is not a problem for him. These footnotes are important.

While I share some of Susan Cole's concerns about the meaning of some pornography, I do not think that her approach adequately deals with all of it. Like all the other genres of mass culture and media, pornography includes a wide range of values and meanings. There is a certain amount of benign, even positive, pornography that validates sexual curiosity, eroticism, mutuality, exploration, and indeed, responsibility.

But there's a lot more material that is ordinarily sexist in its values, especially the kind usually found in men's magazines. Ordinary sexism is bad, and it too has its range. But it permeates the entire culture around us, from *Seventeen* magazine to "Three's Company." It's not different from these, but actually similar. And it shades into the truly brutal, misogynist, and violent. This kind of misogyny, found in *Hustler* magazine and in scenarios of rape and torture, is also found in all kinds of non-explicitly sexual mainstream work and lies at the heart of a certain horror, crime, and "splatter" genre. It's parallelled by — and a product of — the same social illness that produces magazines like *Soldier of Fortune*. If we look at pornography this way, we can see that the way we "deal" with it has to fit within a larger context of how we deal with culture and cultural representation.

I disagree with the premise that all forms of sexual representation will inevitably reinforce heterosexism and patriarchy. But I'm not going to talk about strategies for sexual representation. These are being elaborated today by pro-feminist cultural producers and will blossom providing we can fight for the legal and social conditions that allow them to prosper.

I feel an urgent need to get to the real conditions that produce the sexist values in pornography and the terrible working conditions under which women are exploited and, indeed, brutalized. Let's talk about these, because we can't count on the government to implement a censorship agenda guided by feminist principles even if we could agree on what those principles are — which we cannot.

One of the reasons we have the kind of pornography that we do is because sexuality is ghettoized in society, especially for women. Cathy spoke very articulately about the way women are divided from one another: the sexual versus the asexual, the maternal versus the whore. This kind of division creates boundaries that wrap around pornography and get expressed by it. There is a gold mine of anxiety about sex in our society, and commercial pornography mines it. If we want to get rid of the ghetto in which sex is found, if we want women to have the option of being gregariously sexual in a celebratory way as opposed to having to sell sex under terrible conditions and in the service of sexism, then we have to change the conditions in the culture and at the economic level.

The last article of *Women Against Censorship* is called "Beyond Despair." Perhaps it won't take you beyond despair every day, but I'd like to review some of the major areas of work it recommends because I think it's at these levels that action and change are most important.

To begin with, the fight around employment and economics is crucial — full employment, equal pay, affirmative action, and changes in education and training — the kinds of issues raised by sex trade workers at this conference. The fact remains that if a woman doesn't have an economic choice, then she has to do what she has to in order to survive. Any program dealing with pornography and prostitution that does not take this as its fundamental starting point is, as far as I'm concerned, bankrupt. Any strategy, including a feminist strategy, that diverts attention from this is dangerous and counterproductive.

More directly with respect to sexual representation and cultural work: Edward Donnerstein and James Check, working at the University of Wisconsin and York University respectively, do behavioural and attitudinal research on the effects of different kinds of pornography. They have both found that although young men watching violent pornography do undergo certain attitudinal changes toward women and consent, when they are "debriefed" — that is, when they undergo an educational process whereby they learn about the process of making pornography, about the cultural presence of the "rape myth" and the way its values are present in what they've seen — their understanding of issues of consent and women's dignity is then found to be greater than that of comparable groups of men who have not undergone this experience.

In other words, the attitudinal harms brought about by exposure to certain kinds of material can be undone through education, and indeed, the process of exposure and analysis can be positively beneficial and empowering. This means that with the exception of people who are brutalized to the point where they are not in control of their behaviour, people — yes, even men — are capable of learning and rethinking their attitudes with the proper amount of education.

This means that an anti-censorship position requires that we get serious about education. We need to have a different kind of sex education, not only in the schools but also among adults in the community. It has to include artists and performers who provide expressive vehicles that validate respect, consent, and mutuality as they validate eroticism and plurality. We need sex education that talks about the kinds of issues people actually confront in their sex lives and not simply sperms and ova and family studies. This needs to be part of a much larger campaign of media literacy in the schools in which we teach young people to understand how mass media is produced and what kinds of values it, usually implicitly, conveys.

A few years ago the National Action Committee on the Status of Women (NAC) proposed to the Applebaum-Hébert commission on the arts that women needed a television station of their own. Since then that recommendation has disappeared into a sea of concern about other kinds of issues, including the legal suppression of pornography. In a number of important ways we are now in some sense even further behind in terms of access to the mass media or having control over our own. And our ability to force public cultural programming on sexuality along the lines I've described is about zero. It's time to put energy into fighting in the mainstream and organizing our own media to deal with the myriad issues of sexuality within a feminist approach to issues of gender. By the time North American children reach high school, they've spent more time watching television and film than they've spent in school. No amount of censorship of pornography can counteract this kind of education. The only thing that can is education and the existence of a different kind of television and film.

Finally we have to fight to defend those who are under attack. I don't have to speak for the sex trade workers — they've spoken for themselves. But I can speak for feminists as a feminist. We must defend prostitutes and strippers against victimization as part of our larger feminist commitment. We must defend our gay brothers and sisters and their right to their own sexuality and sexual culture. Let us not permit feminist concern about violence against women to allow the state to carry out an anti-feminist agenda.

The submissions to the Fraser Committee in 1984 represented a stage in feminist discussion about pornography in which the position Susan Cole represents was clearly the majority line, so to speak, of the feminist movement. As I've indicated, there have been important shifts since then. It's crucial that women whose views have changed in this debate now speak out and act in accordance with their current ideas. And it's also crucial that women look at what has actually happened since that time — in terms of the wording of proposed legislation, the action of the courts, and the behaviour of customs agents, provincial censor boards, and police forces vis à vis sexual representation. I think this kind of examination will show that if we — all feminists — want to have the conditions to produce the multiplicity of visions of sexuality that actually represent us, it's at the level of changing economic and cultural conditions, and not at the level of censorship, that we'll have to work.

UNDER THE GUN

Marie Arrington

FIRST OF ALL, I WOULD like to say that the Alliance for the Safety of Prostitutes does not speak for prostitutes. We are an organization and a network of women that includes prostitutes and non-prostitutes. Let me make it clear that there are as many views about prostitution within the sex trade as there are about feminism within the women's movement.

One of the issues that we hear constantly at our speaking engagements with the public is, "What are the effects of prostitution and pornography on society's perception of women?" One more time it's turned around. We think the real question is, "What effect does society's perception of women have on prostitution and pornography?" We think this is the *real* issue because the perception is there before the imagery of the trade comes into being.

Despite the efforts of women struggling for years to equalize our position in society, we are not anywhere near our goal. We do not have economic equality, our share of political power, safe and effective birth control, guaranteed access to safe abortion, adequate health care, or physical safety. In fact, in the last few years we have seen a downslide of women's power, both socially and economically. They allow a few of us to get on top, but it's on the rest of our backs that they do.

At the conference marking the end of the UN Decade of Women, held in Nairobi, the academics were talking about female sexual slavery and how to abolish it. They demanded that the governments of various countries do something about the immigration of women for the sex trade, female sexual slavery, how to get women out of it, how to reform these women, how to educate them about self-esteem. Meanwhile the women at the grass-roots level, who were mostly Women of Colour, were talking about racism, feeding our children, and the economic power of women or lack thereof.

Let me say here that there is an incredible amount of racism in the sex trade at the street level. Women of Colour are in a majority on the street. It is a very clear example of the racism in this society that they even have to be in the industry. Women of Colour are the last hired, the first fired of all women. They cannot get jobs. Many are immigrants and, of course, have to be running the most. They cannot get into the escort services because of the racism in this society and because, of course, the services have to explain to the trick over the phone that this is a Woman of Colour. So it's next to impossible to get into the escort services because none of the men want the women unless it's for kinky sex. There is one escort service in Vancouver that hires Women of Colour, but it has them all advertised and labelled: Black women: "earthy"; Latinos: "hot"; Orientals: "submissive." It reflects how this society functions.

In Vancouver 50 percent of the women on the street are Women of Colour. In Calgary a large percentage are Black and Native women. In Winnipeg it's 80 percent. The police and the Fraser Committee told us it's 98 percent in Regina, mostly Native women. There are many Black women out on the street in Toronto, approximately 60 percent in Montreal. It is not a majority of women in the sex trade who are Third World women.

It is just the majority of those that are on the street and in the prisons. The same is true in the United States from what we hear. Women on the street are viewed as bad girls, and so Women of Colour end up taking that rap.

We are kept apart by the good girl/bad girl thing, as Margo St. James has said. Historically, good girls have been pitted against the bad girls. But men get to decide which label we receive. If we step outside the boundaries, we are already labelled. And the tables can be turned on any of the good girls very fast. One minute you're a good girl, and if you don't do it right, you're a bad girl the next. And what is good in one decade is not necessarily good in the next. Historically, women have built cities through prostitution, but men have created the situation by which women have had to turn to prostitution in order to build these cities. The next time you go through Athens, think about how prostitutes built that city.

Statistics are depressing. Well, I want to depress you. Five prostitute women have been killed in the last few months of 1985: one in Vancouver, one in Edmonton, one in Toronto, and two in Montreal. I want to depress you even further. In Seattle, Washington, where prostitution is outlawed, more than eighty women have disappeared in the last three or four years. Forty-three bodies have been found. Most of the women were twenty or under, and a majority of them were Black. Margo St. James spoke about racism, noting that the police won't take the information until a white woman or a straight woman is killed. This is very true. In fact, the police will not take the information about an assault from a prostitute woman unless a straight woman has been assaulted with the same modus operandi. Then they want the prostitute women to come forward and testify.

Society's perception of women dictates that it is the women who are punished for prostitution, while the male customers are condoned. The new law, C-49, states that the men are going to be charged also. Well, good luck. It is our experience that whenever men get busted, the police say, "I won't charge you" or "I won't go to your wife if you testify against the woman," and these men sing a song.

Often people ask, "What kind of women turn to prostitution?" Never do we hear the question, "What kind of men buy prostitutes?" Well, I'll tell you. This is one of my favourite themes. The English Collective of Prostitutes did a survey of a thousand prostitutes. It estimated that 80 percent of all men have been, will be, or are tricks. Look around, you guys. Their survey also found that the more education a man had and the higher his position in this society, the kinkier the sex he likes. These are the men that like "golden showers," humiliation, domination, and all the other things that the rest of society freaks out about. And so do these men on the surface, but not in practice. The same double standard that applies in society shows up in prostitution over and over again. If a man is busted, his record will not follow him around for the rest of his life because so far men have not been given a criminal record for soliciting or being a trick.

In order to have a man convicted of pimping, you have to have a prostitute testify against him. This is not very likely to happen because some of the time a prostitute doesn't see him as a pimp and some of the time he is not a pimp, but a man that is living with a woman and sharing her income, just as many other men are living with women that have straight jobs and share their income with them. But that's not to say that there aren't any pimps. There are many, and we will see an increase in pimping with the passing of Bill C-49. Men are not likely to get their children apprehended if charged. Nor are they likely to have a job refused to them if they are charged because it is very acceptable in our society for a man to be a trick or a pimp.

I grew up on the street and survived in every way I could except for being a prostitute. I want to dispel the myth that all sexually abused women on the street are prostitutes because they're sexually abused. That is not true. That is something the academics use for their little statistics and their little studies. The kids that I know on the street are running from sexual abuse, but they are not turning to prostitution because of sexual abuse. They are turning to prostitution because there are no social services available. Nobody believes them. They need the money because they can't get welfare. Sexual abuse is only an indirect cause of women turning to prostitution.

Society's perception of women creates prostitution, and I define pornography as the images of prostitution. It is the same act put into pictures. What you see in pornographic movies is basically what happens to women in prostitution. Knives are prevalent because knives are not illegal in this country. Guns are, but they are still used against prostitutes. The major difference between pornography and prostitution is that with pornography, the producer of the image makes the lion's share of the money.

We want to get rid of pornography, but not at the expense of women. If you want to get at the pornographers, address the money that these men make; I would guarantee that there would be less pornography if men were making less money off of it. If the millions and billions that Bob Guccioni makes on pornography were taxed heavily and put into social service programs for women, he would produce less of it. The producers of pornography should be penalized, but not through the courts and not through the laws, because when you penalize the pornographers and put them out of business, you also put women out of work.

Working to have pornography outlawed or driven back underground drives women underground. Women in pornography are there because it is safer. You don't have to deal with the tricks. You don't have to deal so much with the violence because it is imagery, unless it's snuff films. If you start driving it underground, I can see more and more women across the world dying. The idea that we can outlaw without consequence is ludicrous to me. To attempt to outlaw the ways women make money and have them survive is impossible unless you have other alternatives.

As much as I don't like to admit it, there are women in this particular profession who say all the time that they are there because they want to be. I personally have a really hard time with this. But maybe there is a reason for it. Working on the issues of pornography and prostitution is top priority for me at this time because I can see women being jailed, losing their children.

I can also foresee straight women being harassed and charged with soliciting under C-49 because it's going to be the policemen who determine who is soliciting. In Montreal, where there's a by-law about this, one policeman drives in a cab, and a paddywagon follows. The policeman says, "Hi! How are you?" to the women that are working and drives on. Then the paddywagon comes and charges the women with soliciting. In court it's the policeman's word against theirs, and anybody that has had anything to do with the police or works in the sex industry knows the police lie. I'm not going to tell you that they sometimes bend the truth; I'm telling you that they lie. It is deliberate, and they have admitted it, and they have said, "So prove it."

We are saying that all women are under the gun. We see C-49 as a step backwards. It is not an accident that it is happening. It is another form of control and splitting the good girls from the bad girls.

WORKING GIRLS

Valerie Scott

I WORK PRIMARILY as a prostitute, but I also do some work in porn, mostly in live sex and some photography. What a lot of porn workers would like to see is the right to exist, the right to work without being ostracized from society, the right to work without being charged and prosecuted. We would like to see the obscenity laws taken away, and we'd like people to be able to make up their own minds about what they consider to be obscene.

We also think that an organization should be set up for actors and actresses who work in porn, similar to ACTRA, which is for the "legitimate" actors and actresses so that we could have pensions, disability insurance, dental plans, et cetera. And we would also be able to set a minimum pay scale and standards for working conditions.

This is where we are coming from on this. We don't think pornography is going to go away, just as we don't think prostitution is going to go away. And what we are basically saying is, let us take care of ourselves. We're perfectly capable of doing it. We have been doing it for years under the most distressing conditions. And until you allow us to exist, we'll still be working under distressing conditions. We want to be able to work and control our business and our lives by ourselves.

From the Floor

PARTICIPANT 1: I THINK what you're saying is wonderful — the most positive thing I've heard yet at a convention or gathering in terms of our perspective. And I really want to walk forward with that positive thing, but I do have to go back to making shit. Susan, I have some problems with you. I listened to you talk and use the fact that we're violated in our work environment to give some sort of legitimacy to your argument. You've made it very clear that you don't want to talk to politicized whores or politicized porn workers. This is the problem that we've been facing continually. You only use the gutter stories to back up your position. Let's stop the victim shit. What Varda is talking about is, let's recognize that we're not crippled as women in this industry. We are capable of exercising a healthy control over our own environment.

SUSAN G. COLE: I believe you, but I also believe what other women say. I really think it's important to understand that there are women being hurt. You can defend prostitutes' rights to work and still recognize that women are getting hurt. You can support the decriminalization of prostitution and still recognize that women are getting hurt. We can do this, but no one, not even a member of the sex trade, is going to silence me from talking about what is happening to other women.

PARTICIPANT 2: But you're not giving legitimacy to our story of how we're being hurt and who is hurting us. You — with your unwillingness to contact us — *you*'re hurting us. I don't see what good you've done for me when I've experienced violence because you're talking as a fucking observer. I *know* fucking violence. You sit on your little pedestal. And I can't come to you as a politicized whore and say, "I've been hurt like this, and this is who did it." You don't like my definition of who's doing it, and so you don't want to hear my story.

PARTICIPANT 3: If you watch videos, or if you go to your local movie theatre where mainstream movies are being shown, you will see that there's rape, there's violence against women, there's degradation. That's a part of life that we live with right now. And yes, it's like all other sexism; it's part of all other sexism. But women who are shown as being not very bright in ads, shown as dumb housewives — that is not the same thing as showing them being tortured and killed for someone's sexual stimulation. They're a continuum.

In the last ten years, increasingly in pornography and in the mainstream media, women are depicted as subhuman people, people who should be tortured and killed, people who aren't worthy of respect. This is not simply a symptom of what's going on. I think it's part of producing what's going on. It's teaching men in particular, who may be very angry about where they are in society, upset that they're not employed. Who is to blame? If you read pornography, it says, "She thinks she's something. I'll show her that she's not." There's always an element of discipline, of teaching there. In Germany the Nazis taught that the Jews were responsible for the economic problem. Likewise, pornography is saying women are responsible; moreover, they're subhuman, so it doesn't really matter what you do to them.

I've been raped. I live with the fear every day of that possibility happening to me. And when I look at magazines that show women being tortured and killed, I don't say, "That's a fantasy, that's something no one would ever do." I say that's a real possibility that could happen to me, and someone's teaching someone about their sexuality, and they could use that against me. If we don't believe that pornography affects people, why would we believe that an alternative media affects people? Furthermore, a billion dollars a year are spent on pornography. Most women's groups can't scrape up enough money to put out little newsletters, never mind present alternative images.

I think it's very important that we do something about violent pornography. I agree that under the current laws there's no guarantee that they won't be used against homosexuals or feminists, but the laws exist now. You can make the law very specific. You can say that the torture and killing of people for sexual stimulation is not acceptable. You can put in a provision saying that homosexuality doesn't reside under the law. And I think everyone should fight to make sure that the law does not have the things in it that they want to be protected. The time is now to work on developing a law that protects women, protects gays, protects everyone who would like to speak out. It's not the time to say, "Well, there's no need to change the laws. There's no need to do anything about it. We'll just try to present alternative images."

VARDA BURSTYN: Maybe I should clarify a few things. I never said pornography had no effect. I know that anything that is there in the culture and that expresses a view communicates something. Otherwise, why bother even discussing it? What I said is that there isn't an absolute, direct relationship between pornography and violence against women. That's one thing. Second, I never said that violent pornography is the same as advertising. I said violent pornography is the same as *Dressed to Kill*, which is a violent movie. Third, if Crosbie is going to take the one draconian measure out of the Fraser Report's recommendations on prostitution and ignore all the other stuff, what makes you think that you are going to have any effect on how he uses other things?

What I'm suggesting to you is to look at the evidence and see what the various apparatuses of power are doing with feminist concerns. They are not taking them and implementing them. They can't. If you want to have a judiciary or a censor board that is able to look at material in a particular way, it has to be made up of feminists, lesbians, gay men, transsexuals, prostitutes, and sex workers. Then maybe I would consider a censor board. But then if you could have such a thing, you wouldn't need a censor board because then you would have a state that represents the majority.

PARTICIPANT 4: Valerie Scott, you said earlier regarding both prostitution and pornography, "We want to be left alone, and we'll take care of business ourselves." Organized crime may want to be left alone to take care of business itself, but I don't want it to. You have to give me an explanation of why you should be left alone to take care of business yourself.

PARTICIPANT 5: As prostitutes, for one thing, we are not organized crime. It's a very bad analogy.

VALERIE SCOTT: It's not like theft. It's not, as Cathy said, organized crime. And you probably have a right to your job. So why can I not organize myself? Why do I have to be continually oppressed?

PARTICIPANT 4: I don't want the government to say, "Leave us alone, public. Stay out of it. This is government business." I don't want the government to do that.

VALERIE SCOTT: Well, we're going to have to organize ourselves and govern ourselves. We can't have the government governing us as prostitutes, and we certainly can't have you.

PARTICIPANT 6: It seems to me that the underlying difference in this discussion is, in fact, a different attitude on the part of different feminists toward the state and how much of an ally it can be of ours in the present context and how much it can't be. If people address that point and we're clear on it, the heat in this discussion would be less because we would actually be clear on where we're coming from.

VARDA BYRSTYN: I'm going to attempt to turn the heat into light on my end. Two feminists yesterday used the term *social control*. We have to find a balance between social control and freedom of expression. My socialist-feminist hackles rose at the term *social control* because the state is not a simple institution. It's a complex institution that has many different aspects, it has many different tendencies within it. The Canada Council can, if we're lucky, fund some feminist art that then the Toronto police will bust in the window of a Queen Street store. So we've got different things within it, but overall it represents, in crystallized form and in the form of power, the interests of the dominant strata or the dominant classes in society. This is why, despite the 90 percent consensus at the time of the Fraser Committee on pornography, we are not going to see a feminist agenda coming from John Crosbie. Social control talks about state control. *Freedom of expression*, as people have pointed out before, is a term that's really ignored a lot of women's experience.

What I would like us to talk about is social empowerment, or self-determination. I'm non-pornography — I mean I'm neither one nor the other. I'm not for social control, and I'm not for the liberal notion of freedom of expression. I'm in favour of a sense of community where people determine what they want to do and how they want to do things. The difference would be between an agency that runs the lives of prostitutes and street kids and an agency that makes money and resources available to street kids and prostitutes to do what they want with. It's a very basic difference, but in the bureaucracies it's a fundamental difference in terms of how things work. So for me the state is a capitalist and a patriarchal state, and that's why it's not going to do anything but take what it can out of our concerns to legitimize itself, but not work in our interests.

SUSAN G. COLE: I have to confess a lot more ambivalence about what I think our relationship is to the state. And I am very interested in an exploration of an ambivalence that leaves room for the view that the power embodied in the state is bad, but so is the power that is embodied in all other kinds of institutions and places. My problem with the traditional, so-called anti-censorship view is that I want to leave room for feminists to be able to say, "I'm not sure that this kind of state power is any worse than the traditional power of men within the family institution or anywhere else." Some of us are struggling to figure out what we're willing to trade off. All I know is that I'm trying to find my basis for empowerment so that I can feel empowered somewhere, but I'm not convinced that the state is the worst and most awful repository of power at this time. That's how I'm looking at it, but it's all in a beginning and struggling stage.

PARTICIPANT 7: When those of us who are uncomfortable with censorship or against censorship say that we are, we hear from feminists that we're not looking at the horrors of pornography. And that's always the first thing that people say: "What about pornography? Isn't it bad? What about mutilation?" I don't think that's the first step. We can agree that a movie that really mutilates a woman is very bad and completely disagree over strategy. And this discussion is about strategy. The thing that pisses me off about the side of the debate that Susan represented today is that you don't let it be that. You try to take it away from the question of strategy and say, basically, that we're not being feminist enough, that we're not sensitive enough to the horrors of male sexism and things like that. How do we think social change is going to happen? Why do we think pornography exists, and how will it change? I don't think that legislation and censorship is going to get rid of pornography. If I did, if I thought that it was possible to get rid of pornography by calling on government to get rid of it, then I might feel differently.

SUSAN G. COLE: I have made a point of saying that one of the struggles we've had is that we keep being put into camps. I think it's a drag that anti-censorship feminists and men are accused of not taking violence against women seriously. I'm a little distressed about this notion that anybody thinks censorship is going to get rid of pornography. Nobody ever said rape laws were going to end rape. Nobody ever said welfare was going to end poverty. I am opposed to obscenity and censorship. I'm interested in a legal remedy that will allow women to sue pornographers for the harm that's done to them. I do not think that's going to end pornography. I think it's going to give some women some relief. I want to know why, when the subject is sexually explicit material, whatever small little thing we want to do is supposed to solve all the problems of sexism. I wonder why Varda thinks that if we're working on this issue, we don't care about the other ones, or it's distracting us from our real goals. I know she wouldn't say that about the pro-choice movement. Why is she saying it about those of us who are dealing with violence against women?

PARTICIPANT 8: When people talk about the state, would you also like to abolish the laws against sexual assault? That's the power of the state. Do you want to abolish the laws against equal pay for work of equal value? That's the power of the state. Do you want to abolish human rights commissions, which I've heard gay activists not only want to keep but also want to expand, to include people discriminated against by reason of sexual preference? I've heard small businessmen refer to human rights commissions as a "human rights Gestapo." What it comes down to is: you're for the power of the state when it's something you want, like equal pay for work of equal value or laws against sexual assault. And for people who claim to be against the power of the state, it has nothing to do with the power of the state. They just don't want laws regulating violent pornography, and they should say that.

PARTICIPANT 1: The censorship law is really saying to that woman that you don't care about her. Linda Lovelace didn't start coming forward until feminists gave the message that we care about you. If you have censorship, you're saying to that woman in that film or in that magazine that you don't want to see her, you don't want to know her name, you don't want to know her life. And she will never, as long as she is getting that message, go into a court of law and say, "That producer hurt me." And until we're willing to look at the women who are being directly violated and give them the power and the message to go into that courtroom, we are never going to get to the bottom of this. I hear anti-pornography feminists saying one thing to me: they don't like my cunt and what I do with it.

VARDA BURSTYN: Because in my view the state is not a simple mechanism for public authority to bring in what we want, we need to have that kind of intelligent attitude that says we want laws that will help us where they can, and we don't want laws that can be used against us. It's not really an inconsistency; it's just smart to do it that way. We are in a process of social change, and if we don't get our gains rolled back, and if we can succeed over the next few generations in the kind of struggle that we've been in now for about 150 years, over time, with luck, it will reflect itself in the constitution of public authorities that we would call the state. At that time there will be a different relationship between something like the women's movement and a state.

But right now that's not the way things are. The way things are, we have primarily a patriarchal state, also a capitalist state, and a series of movements including the feminist movement. We do not want to put something into the hands of the state that it can then use against us. To talk about sexually explicit imagery, even if we put in certain kinds of criteria, will allow that kind of repression. They're not all the same, and we shouldn't lump them all together. Let's think about what we want and go for it, and let's not give anybody, or any agency within that state, a chance to repress us.

Sex Trade Workers and Feminists: Myths and Illusions

An interview with
Amber Cooke

LAURIE BELL: DURING YOUR eighteen years as a professional stripper, what was your perception of your place in the culture of the sex trade and within the wider dominant culture?

AMBER COOKE: I had always believed feminism to be personal empowerment, and the choice to be a stripper — to be my own boss, to be my independent power source, to be creative, to express myself fully, without terms of bureaucracy or established norms — was in fact personally empowering. The women who were in this trade supported each other in finding themselves and empowering themselves in whatever undeveloped aspects or areas they chose, unhampered by a particular value system outside that world. So it was the value system in that world that actually enabled us to empower each other.

LAURIE BELL: Many feminists might feel that within the culture of the sex trade there's no place for women to have personal empowerment.

AMBER COOKE: That's not so. That may be the perception of an outsider, but for women involved in it, there is a whole different

---

reality. The business is run by capitalists, people who want to make a profit, so of course it's set up to their advantage. The whole situation — from the dressing rooms to the stage presentations to the sound system to the lighting system to the practice of paying star status to the money received — are all set up by men for profit. But what the women actually do, our work, while it is under their jurisdiction, is still up to us. So yes, our work is controlled, but what we do when we work isn't.

LAURIE BELL: How much control do the men in the audience have over the women who are stripping?

AMBER COOKE: No control at all. Although with table-dancing they have some control. But table-dancing, once it was brought back, gave power to the audience. Now they can pick and choose who they want to come and dance at their table, and of course the competition is great because wages have been cut. And so to make your wages up, you have to then pamper the male in whatever he chooses for you to do. But when there are stage shows and only stage shows, the power is outside of their hands and in the hands of the woman. She embraces it, she puts forth what she sees as entertainment and erotic. And they're the audience.

LAURIE BELL: In society as sexist as the one we find ourselves in, do you think the men that are in the audience can distinguish between real women and strippers as an act, as entertainment?

AMBER COOKE: Sure they know that. The struggle for male and female roles right now in our society is very difficult. It's painful as you grasp new inner truths and try to deal externally with them and with whoever your partner or co-workers may be. But to come to a strip club — of course it's a fantasy. Reality is outside the door; this is now fantasy. This is a place in which to relax and not have to worry about all of what it takes in relating your identity with reality and co-operating with others. So they get to come in and put that aside. They know that they are interacting with the women outside the door — their wives, their sisters, their daughters, their mothers — in a fuller capacity. They know the difference.

LAURIE BELL: What about the accusation that seeing strippers and looking at porn sets up unrealistic expectations in men of their wives or their partners? Things that women at home can't live up to?

AMBER COOKE: I can't see that as the problem of pornography. I can see the problem of men relating to women. All of us can go to any media — movies, shows, books — and if we base our real-life interactions with people on any of that, we're going to be mistaken; we are going to come out short in the end. I don't believe that pornography contributes to that. It is men's responsibility as human beings to relate to women as whole human beings.

LAURIE BELL: As a child it is hard to see teachers as whole people. You see them only in the role of teacher. Isn't it a bit the same with women working as strippers? It's very hard for me to imagine them outside of that role. How do they live? Who do they relate to? Do they have friends? There's been such a stigma about women who work in the sex trade that the rest of us never meet them in our daily lives.

AMBER COOKE: You probably do all the time but just don't know it. When you're very young, you don't have a full sense of self yet, so to look at a person and imagine their full sense — of course it's difficult; it's beyond your consciousness. But as you become aware of who you are and what your destiny is, especially as a teenager, when you start to realize your own sexual desires, your own sexual struggle, you can realize that other people have that too. The more aware you are of yourself, the more you can understand that other people have other aspects you might not see. When you sit down and think about it, you know that everyone has a life. These people don't just magically come to life once they're on stage or in a club.

LAURIE BELL: Because the sex trade is kept as a separate subculture, one of the consequences seems to be that people in the dominant culture have no idea about the lives of women working in the sex trade.

AMBER COOKE: Yes, and that's partially created by the women in the sex trade themselves. They want to create a great deal of that isolation, that barrier, for their own protection. So as much as the dominant society wants to look the other way so that it doesn't have to deal with this whole group of people that it doesn't understand, we try to keep it away too. As soon as it gets hold of some information or knowledge, there's books written, there's articles written — there's all kinds of information coming out distorted through society's own biases. Not from what our life actually is. So yes, we want to protect ourselves from the curiosity, the exploitation, the thrill seekers who are just going to take a peek and then use their own imagination from there.

LAURIE BELL: How safe is it for a woman to work as a stripper in this city?

AMBER COOKE: A lot safer than being a hooker. A lot safer. Politicians and the law still keep the women as sitting ducks though. They can still come into a club and enforce "indecent acts" or "obscene acts"; they have various by-laws under which they can charge the woman, but it's up to their discretion. And now that they've made the taking off of the G-string your "option" (although it's not your option — it's mandatory if you want work), to take it off means that you are at the mercy of the whim of anyone that comes in and chooses to fine you or charge you. So power has been taken away from the woman and put with the audience, with the club owners, and with the police. No longer does the woman run her own business.

LAURIE BELL: If you could ask the feminist movement, the women's movement, for things on behalf of women who work in the sex trade, what would they be? What needs to be said to feminists on behalf of women in the sex trade?

AMBER COOKE: We need a multi-faceted solution. It's not as simple as what we need support for or what we need changed. It's not one or two issues. The women in the sex trade themselves need consciousness-raising. They need to be able to understand that they have the ability to change things. They feel that they're powerless because managements keep any talk of organizing outside of the doors. If you are found to be one that wants to unite the people or bring them together, to change something, to change the law, or to strike in a club, to picket a club, or to take a club owner to court for not paying you, you're not hired. You're blackballed. You get a mark against you. So it has to start with women understanding that they have the power.

LAURIE BELL: And do you think feminists can be useful with that?

AMBER COOKE: They can be, but they haven't been so far.

LAURIE BELL: Part of what's being suggested here is that feminists should get to know sex trade workers, that they should lend their support to sex trade workers, and that sex trade workers are as legitimately a part of what we have called the feminist or women's movement as any other women.

AMBER COOKE: More so than some. We've been out there doing our own thing, fighting all the fights that you possibly can to be females in any way we choose, and that's our right and our power. We were out there doing it long before the feminists came in and started picketing clubs, saying that we were exploiting ourselves. We've been self-employed people with our own social aid, our own society, our own system for a long time, based on our power as women. And then the feminists come in and want to fight us. Now in getting them to support us, we have to train them not to fight us! That's one of the first steps.

LAURIE BELL: So perhaps the question really is: What do sex trade workers have to offer feminists or the women's movement?

AMBER COOKE: Betty Friedan says that every woman has the right to say yes and no. You've got to have the choice to say yes or no to what job you're going to have and to your sexuality. It's up to the woman herself. I can't see a group of women coming in, calling themselves feminists, who are ready to put into gear a structure as oppressive as the male structure. And claim that they are in fact helping these women out.

LAURIE BELL: How do you think sex trade workers can get that message to feminists?

AMBER COOKE: I just keep thinking that if feminists could understand that we in fact want to do this work and then enable us to do so. Every time a feminist agency or organization does come to our assistance, it helps a little bit. Once the women understand that they can go to feminists, because the feminists understand what sort of information they're receiving, and once the feminists learn to define the problems of the women in the sex trade — once we have an open dialogue and good communication, we will be putting the power back into the women's hands. I think that's the only way to do it.

LAURIE BELL: But for a woman who works in an escort service or on the street — when she hears the word "feminist," what do you think that brings to mind?

AMBER COOKE: Most of them have an impression that feminists are asexual women. In feminist politics there has to be more than just cut-and-dried intellectualizing and theorizing about what should be and shouldn't be. We need to deal with what *is*, and instead of relating to the women in the sex trade through the rhetoric or the theory, understand the women.

LAURIE BELL: Some feminists think that the best thing that they can do for these women is to help them get out of the trade.

AMBER COOKE: Why?

LAURIE BELL: Because they say women are getting hurt there, women are being exploited, women are spending their lives and their work being at the service of men.

AMBER COOKE: That's their judgment. These people choose to do that. As women. It's like the Roman Catholic judge who wants to base laws on his particular belief of what sin and corruption are. You can't do that. You can't walk in and be that person that says, "Based on my beliefs, everyone has to do this. It has to be my way because this is my value system." You can't do that.

LAURIE BELL: Do you think that feminists are placing a moral judgment on sex trade workers?

AMBER COOKE: I think they're transferring their fears. Most women in one way or another understand the power of their sexuality. But a lot of women are afraid of that power, of how to hold that power, of how to use that power. And when they are confronted with someone who's comfortable doing that, it shakes them up. It challenges them. It makes them question themselves. When that happens, you become threatened and defensive; you react on that basis. The woman who is happy with her sexuality, quite satisfied to embrace it, embark on it, dance with it, enjoy it, then becomes the feared person. I don't believe it's so much morals as it is fear. That's why I say feminists are new at this. They're just coming along saying, "Own your own sexuality," whereas we've been doing it for a long time. We haven't been making a big deal out of it — just doing it.

LAURIE BELL: For you there is no contradiction between a woman being a stripper and a feminist at the same time.

AMBER COOKE: How are they different? It's like saying this mammal is a cat. Same thing. You can be a stripper and a stalwart feminist, you can be a feminist and a stripper — it goes hand in hand. I know women who are feminists who don't understand what it is to embrace their own power. It's only an intellectual concept for them that they are struggling constantly to achieve. I know women in the sex trade who don't struggle to embrace their own power either. They're women who seek their approval from outside sources. That's the struggle for all women. If there's a common denominator that would bring us all together, it is that we are all learning to seek our own approval, especially in terms of sexuality. That's our bond. Wherever you're coming from, you are not exempt from that common denominator.

LAURIE BELL: Has working on the pornography and prostitution conference, being at the conference, working with the Elizabeth Fry Society affected your perceptions of feminism?

AMBER COOKE: It's given me the opportunity to see that feminists actually want to help. There's a real concern there. How founded their concerns are, and the perspective from which those concerns are viewed, is something else again. But we all need education and training. I need training to understand why the feminist takes her stand and how that works for her, and she needs to know that about me.

LAURIE BELL: What do you think could be a good way for that exchange to happen?

AMBER COOKE: That's difficult. A conference is very good. More public talks, more public speeches, more shows. Right now it's at the stage of this brand-new relationship. We're developing trust. That's what we really should be doing right now. All the ways in which you develop trust should be put into gear and acted on. Once there is open communication and trust established, then both of us can know better how to help the other. But right now this is a very, very new thing; it's very tender and gentle. And rather than get into the militant stage much before it's time, let's just develop that trust through books, the media, getting people to talk.

LAURIE BELL: What about the more informal gatherings? It seems that the conference, because of its public nature, was a disadvantage to sex trade workers. It was risky for them to come and identify themselves as sex trade workers.

AMBER COOKE: That's not the real problem, that's not the problem that kept them from being there. The women who are political, who are sex trade activists, are a very small handful of women. And they'll come to all these public talks; they'll keep coming. The names will keep popping up all the time. But women who are out there, who are on the borderline, who are fighting for survival, have not yet been able to indulge themselves, or afford the opportunity, to develop a political analysis. Therefore they see all this political activity around this issue as outside of their realm. They don't understand that they're the living politics of it. Within themselves they're political, but they don't know that they are. They don't know what is happening at these conferences, and they're not ready to come forth and be part of it.

Survival and politics are two different things. Engaging in politics is a luxury, but if you're really, really busy just having to make your money, to keep your ends together, you're going to take all the hours you can to make your money. You're not going to be taking great huge gaps of time for meetings.

If you went out through Toronto and found ten sex trade workers you wanted to talk to, number one, you'd pay them because their time is money. No one's come up with that one yet. Sex trade workers are economically and emotionally vulnerable. It's about their work. And it's been so mishandled so often. It's horrible to come and listen to what people have to say, and their attitudes, and struggle through all that. Especially when it's taking up your time and money. It's a lot easier to walk out the door and go back and do what you're doing with people that know what you're doing. Where everyone isn't standing around analyzing what you're doing and talking about it for hours.

It's the same as any kind of thing with politics and the peasants: keep the peasants so much on the line that thinking about feeding their families is all they have time for. They don't have time for politics — they can't. It's all in somebody else's hands. It doesn't matter which way the politics go — they still have to struggle day after day for food. Put that in the woman's terms too. It doesn't matter what new laws are made, it doesn't matter who shifts power, it doesn't matter what conferences are going on or not going on — she still has to make her bucks.

Say you came out on the street and said, "I'll offer you affordable housing if we can get a thousand of you together this

Saturday afternoon. You'll all sign a petition, and you'll all get an apartment that you can afford to live in." They would be there. That's practical. Sitting around and talking about what they're doing for hours and hours isn't practical.

LAURIE BELL: Do women in the sex trade want to see some sort of tangible support from feminists? Is this the way the feminists need to go in order to make alliances with women in the sex trade?

AMBER COOKE: Absolutely. How were any of the great unions in the States made? People didn't just go around and talk to workers; they went out there and worked with them. They'd live with them. The organizers would help the dying babies. And once the organizers know the life of the people and are with the people, then they can go and make changes because then you have the people's support.

So far everyone is just talking about the sex trade. Practical manoeuvres are needed. Come to their court cases, come to their houses, come to their lives, get involved with them, help them to help themselves. Practical manoeuvres. With the whores it's pretty cut and dried: it all really revolves around C-49 right now. With the strippers it's altogether different.

LAURIE BELL: How is a feminist supposed to get to know a stripper? Where do we meet each other?

AMBER COOKE: What are your likes and dislikes? What do you do in your spare time?

LAURIE BELL: Go to meetings, just like your average feminist! Chances are that I'm not going to meet strippers or hookers at meetings.

AMBER COOKE: It depends on the meetings. Go to a few Al-Anon meetings. You'll meet some. Join the Beat the Street literacy campaign. Go to places where they would go to. I have a friend who spends all day Sunday in church; she plays the organ. You could go to her church and talk to her between sermons. A lot of the women have children. Go to day care centres, meet the moms. Where would you meet any woman? We don't have clubs for strippers only. We work in public places. Go into a club and buy her a drink; say that you just want to talk to her.

LAURIE BELL: In the United States, at least, there seem to be women-only escort services and strip clubs run by women for women. It seems like there's no big deal about it there.

AMBER COOKE: We've received our greatest support from the lesbian community because they are fully supportive of recreational sex; the sex between them is not procreative. So they've backed us 100 percent. Sure, sex is fun. We know that. Never mind babies. Sure.

I think guilt about recreational sex is the overriding issue. Each one of us carries a little piece of that. When we sit down and confront one another, our fears keep coming up. People fear women in the sex trade because they don't understand what that little switch is that they've turned on that makes it okay for sex to be just for fun or a commodity to sell. They don't understand how they've taken away the guilt of the church or the rest of the culture to see it in a much clearer perspective. It may not match your morality system, but sex trade workers are much more clear on what sex is for them.

LAURIE BELL: Are women forced into the sex trade?

AMBER COOKE: There are women working as waitresses, as legal secretaries, as librarians, as nurses, and that may be the only thing they can do. So that's what they're going to do. And then there's women who celebrate in their occupation or careers. It's the same with women in the sex trade. Some feel they are victims. Some *are* victims. And then there are also others who have made that choice and celebrate that choice. We're not so different.

The whole difference is viewing sex as a commodity or as recreation or as entertainment. When you take sex out of the traditional, intimate bonding process, it becomes something else.

LAURIE BELL: And that's okay?

AMBER COOKE: Of course! How many things in our lives are totally acceptable because they bring us pleasure? Most things are supposed to be means to an end. Take the Catholic view of sex as strictly procreative. I'd rather be a whore than a Catholic.

People will actually pay for sex, and that makes it a valuable commodity to a woman. That's her right. As long as people are willing to buy sex, there will be people who choose to make their living in the sex trade. Unless we return to the temple prostitutes, who did it for God.

LAURIE BELL: It has been said that the women's movement won't really be a women's movement unless it includes whores.

AMBER COOKE: Absolutely. There are a lot of whores that are there; they just don't state that they are. So let's get honest about this. And how can any women's movement be a true representation of women without representing all women?

Whatever level of political consciousness women in the sex trade are at, the best thing for them is to be matching up with a group of women in the feminist movement who are open to them and can do something to support them. So even apart from the infighting on both sides of this issue, the networking has to be done very carefully or we are going to be throwing ourselves even further into their chaos.

Sex trade workers don't want much more than anybody else out there doing their work. They want working conditions that are hygienic and conducive to doing their business. They want money for the work they do. One of the things that all feminists could do for all sex trade workers is really simple: make sure that the health standards for the dressing rooms are up to scratch. Ensure that there is a toilet, that there is some sort of ventilation, and that there are heat and light. Those are really basic things, yet the working women can't get it for themselves.

Go into a club and find out what kind of air system they have to get rid of the smoke so we're not all choking and going blind in there. Go down to the dressing rooms and get rid of all the drips that force you to wear something on your feet all the time because the floor's wet. There's no proper light, there's no place to hang up your clothes, so they sit on the back of the chair and fall into these puddles. That would be a good place to start because then the women would know you're on their side. When they don't have pneumonia that winter, they'll remember the feminists.

REALISTIC FEMINISTS

An interview with

Valerie Scott, Peggy Miller, and Ryan Hotchkiss

of the Canadian Organization for the Rights of Prostitutes (CORP)

CORP: THE ONE issue that everyone is running away from in this whole discussion of prostitution is anonymous sex. At the heart of this is the whole business of not being involved in monogamy, the whole business of treating our sexuality and giving it the same kind of credibility and support as we would any of our other needs. We somehow isolate that, and we want to get feminists talking about the heart of the issue, which is sex.

Let's for once put aside the whole business of the environment in which we are now forced to operate. Feminists are hiding behind that environment and using it to reinforce their own value system and their own morality, and they're not confronting their sexuality. They have in the past joined with the Moral Majority. It started at the turn of the century, as a matter of fact, when the whole thing was going down for the vote. It was prior to that, that whores were allowed to walk around, and there weren't a lot of laws around whoring. Then to try to get another image of woman and support her in her endeavour to become other things in the world, the feminists got into bed with the Moral Majority and supported all of these laws that we're now having to operate under. And they have since been using that corrupt environment that they've helped shape against us to support the argument that prostitution is corrupt. That's when the shit started to happen.

One of the ways that feminists traditionally do this is by hiding behind the pimp in exploiting us as well. They use the pimp issue and the abuse issue as a way out, always pointing to him and pointing to the way we have to work as being very corrupt, when in fact these laws were the result of prostitutes being ostracized by society in general and specifically feminists.

What we have to get feminists to look at, honestly for once in their fucking lives (and I say "fucking lives" because they *do* fuck, these madonnas), is their own investment in keeping us ostracized. Where is their crown of honour without us to point at? Where's their little reward for being such good girls if it's no longer dishonourable not to keep their legs closed? Where's the ring on their finger as the nice good mother if, in fact, the nice good mother and that whole role is undermined? She's incredibly vested, and even gay women are vested, because they're not really breaking away from the good-girl role. They are going another way, but they still keep that value of a little girl — this is what good girls do. The only reason they get honours and credibility for it and respectability for what they're doing is because we're there.

Once we get rid of the prejudice against whores and the bad girl, that part of feminists' self-image, giving them credibility and validity, is going to be uprooted. They can always lean on that — "At least I'm a nice girl." She can be a sleazeball in every other way, but she'll be treated nicely because she doesn't open her legs except for someone she loves. She can, in fact, be an incredibly deceitful and manipulative wife and abuse her sexual power over the man in the marriage, but she will be a good woman. So all of that will be uprooted for her as soon as we gain credibility. She will have to find some real ways of giving herself validity and not on anyone else's ass. And that's the investment she's got — a lifetime of it, going way back to mommy and grandma and everyone else. And even the gay woman has it.

LAURIE BELL: Isn't it men who really benefit from anonymous sex?

CORP: No. She benefits. She gets her halo, she gets the ring.

LAURIE BELL: How do you benefit from anonymous sex? You open your legs for the patriarchy.

CORP: We open our legs for the money.

LAURIE BELL: Feminists say that anonymous sex only benefits men.

CORP: Anonymous sex has validity in its own right. Since when is sex only acceptable and valid and good sex if it's linked to love or linked to someone that they've invested in, in terms of a relationship? There are a lot of people who feel unwilling or reluctant or unable to express a lot of pockets of their sexuality and their sexual needs unless it is with someone that they don't have to look at afterwards. There's an excitement that goes with a new person, a novelty. These are all things that are accepted when it's expressed in other areas. Needing novelty is perfectly acceptable around other needs that we have. It's perfectly acceptable if we meet someone on a train and we can talk to them in a way that we couldn't talk to a best friend. If it's acceptable for that kind of need, is our sexuality so one-dimensional that we have no need for other ways of expressing it? Is the excitement of novelty somehow dirty when it comes to that? It isn't dirty when we need to have new kinds of friends, new kinds of food, new kinds of clothes, a new look. Sexually we like novelty too. We like a variety of people around us, a variety of ideas.

The sexual act involves so much of us. Everything we are all day long spills over to shape the sexual need we have that night. And it triggers a whole network of other associations going through our life. So the shaping of our sexual need is a kaleidoscope — it's constantly changing. Humanity benefits from giving legitimacy to all kinds of sexual needs as long as they're consentual. We benefit directly because we've given ourselves permission to involve ourselves as the receiver or the giver, depending on how you see the act, and we're able to get a reward for being able to do that. That reward is sort of our contribution to society, and it also supports us.

No one should have to do anything they don't want for a living, but that's not a reality in life. Most of us end up taking jobs where there are certain compromises made, so we make a compromise: we'll give up this many hours of our day (and we've chosen a profession that involves the least hours) for this much reward, and we've chosen a profession that gives the most reward in terms of work hours put in. And we will hopefully have the most control over our work environment: we will be our own boss. So we know that everyone has to do something to make a living; we've chosen the things that to us are the least evil in terms of what we're going to get out of it. We don't think any woman should have to make the choice to work as a prostitute any more than any woman should be forced to work in a factory or forced to be a lawyer or a doctor, for that matter. But we obviously do feel that it's a legitimate service, and we'd like to be able to provide it to all people.

As far as we're concerned, there are a lot of women who could use this kind of service. They've never had a good fuck in their life. They need the service, and it would be well worth the money to pay and have a good service and awaken their sexuality. We think that it's a legitimate service that anyone should be entitled to, and under the most healthy circumstances, with all the resources and support from society that they might need to get the most out of the experience. No woman should have to take on the job she is not wanting to. But we set up an environment that deprives everyone of all of the above.

LAURIE BELL: Is prostitution good in and of itself?

CORP: Of course it is, and this ideal about no anonymous sex is crap. Anonymous sex is as valid as any other kind of sex. So if no anonymous sex is the feminist ideal, then we do not agree with that ideal at all. We don't think that's ideal.

What we keep hearing is that nobody should have to do anything they don't want. That to us is the interpretation of the feminist ideal, and we think that's fine, except that we don't think this world is ever going to come to that.

Is monogamous, twenty-year-old sex the real thing? What is the real thing? And we think the real thing is what works for the individual, and let's allow that individual to have that choice of what is the real thing for them. We don't want anyone telling us what kind of sex we can have, whether it's for money or not. And we certainly wouldn't tell anybody else what kind of sex they could have. We wouldn't go into a meeting of lesbians and say, "Well, we don't think that this kind of sex is right." Or we wouldn't go into a meeting at church and say, "Well, this kind of sex, if you're married and madly in love, is not all right."

The question is, really: is anonymous sex desirable in our ideal world, in reference to a feminist vision? The feminist vision is unhealthy because it is cloning sexuality. What they're trying to do is set up a structure around people's sexuality. They're trying to keep it segregated and pocketed from the other parts of themselves, rather than allowing all of their parts and needs to talk together and respond together. Anytime we're talking about structuring something like this that's so intimately tied with our whole being, we're talking about pocketing and isolating. In creating a dream of an egalitarian society, feminists project on that future the fuck-ups of today. But one of the things that we should know from today is that sex, when it's structured, isn't healthy. We've got to break these codes that set up situations where we're not being spontaneous, where we're not being integrated in ourselves. So the vision to us really calls a lot of things into question.

First of all, it calls into question the feminist understanding of what being human is all about. Second, it is so presumptuous and arrogant to think that we can really clearly imagine an egalitarian society and protect it from today's fuck-ups. What are they doing talking about it?

You asked what our ideal situation is. Our ideal situation is like anybody else's — that we have control over our work environment, we have control over our prices, we make our own compromises. We know what it's worth to us. She doesn't know, he doesn't know — but we know what it's worth to us. We want the support systems everyone else has. Let our businesses go under the same rules that regular businesses go under. Let our businesses have the support of the medical profession, the legal profession. Let us set professional standards. That's our ideal — from our perspective; not every girl feels the same way. It's great when you can sit at home and get a call and go out. You can go out and not feel like you're about to meet someone in some sort of clandestine affair. You never shake those overtones. You're on the way to a date, you feel good, and you're saying, "This is a clandestine affair," and it kind of shapes you. You want to set the price of what the trade-off is worth to you. You want it also to be sensitive to his needs as a person. He's a person. He's not a fucking animal — he's a person! He may just need to be held, he may just need you to act out some fantasy and you don't even touch him, which is something. Let us get something set so that we can be better able to give better service. Lots of guys that we see want to talk. You don't want to be so angry because you're the fall guy for society that you go to him and it's like, "You're a fuck. You're getting away with this" and you can't be sensitive. You want an environment where you can be sensitive.

Imagine therapists trying to give good service to someone if they're seeing them on the side because they could be put in jail, and the guy that's coming has this attitude, "Well, you're just a slut anyway" somewhere in his head because he's been conditioned. "Well, you're just a fucking dirty therapist anyway! I can say anything to you." And the guy is really trying to meet the real needs of this person, and he can't get past the other shit.

Feminists have got to pretend that the vision they have of this wonderful egalitarian society is somehow going to mean that we're all going to be sexual clones. That's the most unhealthy, neurotic, psychotic-producing concept we've heard in a long time, and any therapist will tell you that. We deal with guys needing a lot of help because they've got that idea too. "I'm a bad person because I want my cock sucked." And you listen to them making comments of shame and mixed anger and not knowing what to do because they've got it too. They're people, and we're tired of the feminists treating them like they're not. Egalitarian society? Since when does an egalitarian society exclude men? If this is such a wonderful vision, how come they never ask men about it? Isn't that what egalitarian is all about?

Men have had the power to buy, and women are so busy reacting to that fact that they're not able to distinguish between the wrong distribution of power and wealth and the legitimacy of the needs.

As far as we're concerned, we're the only feminists around. We think whores are more conscious of feminism from a healthy perspective than most other feminists. The reason is that we're constantly interacting with men and conscious of where they're coming from, so in that sense we're really hearing them. And despite all of this we don't lose our focus. Once we've been politicized, we're not losing our focus in terms of understanding where we need to find power and what we have to do.

We have stood against a long history of abuse from other women and said, "Wait a minute. We will set our own sexual standards, and we will not abide by this business of having to marry to get money." We are going to look head on, in a more liberated way than most feminists we know are able to do, at what sexuality is about, what male needs are really all about, what female needs are really all about, and the economy that we have to work within, the commodity system that we have to work in, and we're going to say, "Okay, with all of that, this is fair: we want power to negotiate a trade-off around a real human need (which belongs to women as well; women should be able to find it as well on the same terms), and we're not going to be forced into being good girls and dating guys because we need dinner or marrying because we want security." We're putting it on a level that feminists can't. They still need to fool themselves: "Well, I'm not really lonely. I just want this, or I just want that." You're fucking right they're lonely. If we're lonely, we'll go and trade off something else for it.

We're more realistic feminists. A prostitute is a realistic feminist as opposed to an idealistic, hypocritical, shadowy feminist who doesn't want to confront the facts of life, the facts of her own negotiating and trade-off in the marriage situation, the fact that the male is her brother and not the enemy and the fact that she's afraid of sex.

We've confronted our own need, in a society that's a commodity system, realistically and head on. We have not succumbed to all the pressure to give men what they want on their terms. We've said, "No. You want to fuck. We won't be with you the whole fucking night and put up with that shit. We will be with you for one hour and address your needs, stripped of the garbage, and we'll give it to you head on." We've also said, "No, we won't put up with a marriage and security." Or "No, we won't do this sexual act or that sexual act." Or "We won't be manipulated by you sexually. You'll pay for what you want."

LAURIE BELL: Do you believe feminists have colluded with the rest of society to corrupt what is essentially a good profession, a necessary service?

CORP: Very much so. That comes into where they're pimping us. They're hiding again behind all that façade and all the little fears to make us work in a really dangerous environment to keep our scores down. We think that feminists are right in there with the Moral Majority and all those people. And we feel like dirty shits.

We want feminists to stop pimping our ass. We want them to start listening to us. We want them to stop looking at us as victims and see us as equals. We want them to address sexuality as it really is.

Let's start with theirs. Never mind ours. We want feminists to start looking at their sexuality — honestly. When they get through taking care of their own little rose garden, maybe they can start looking at ours. Maybe we'll be willing to discuss it. But let's take care of your own little garden.

What are feminists paying respect to when they're totally negating an important part of their human needs, when they're supporting all the things that will negate their human needs and other people's human needs? What's respectful about that? What's respectful about a prison where prostitutes are put? Feminists have put sex in a little box in the corner of their minds. What's respectful about keeping anger suffocated and not allowing people to learn how to integrate it into acts where it can come out constructively? What's integrated about thinking that parts of the human body are dirty? What's respectful? You don't feel that your pussy is being respected when you listen to them talk. The message that you get is that our cunts are dirty. Or if it's not our cunts, it's his cock.

Well, we're people. This is the egalitarian vision here. Come on, girls. What's respectful about those things? Who is it respectful to? Better yet, show us the person that's feeling respected. Show us the person that's feeling loved from these messages, because really, it's up to the receiver, isn't it, that they're feeling respected and loved. How can you feel loved when you're being invalidated, or when parts of you are being invalidated? How can you feel respected? That's the test of whether it is all of the above. Ask someone whether they feel it. One thing that's really clear is that feminists usually don't take prostitutes' testimony as valid. You'll get a group of feminists from northern Canada coming down to talk about conditions in a mining town, and there doesn't seem to be a problem accepting those women's testimony about their life as valid without having to interpret it. But when you have a prostitute that says, "Well, I don't agree with the way you're interpreting my life, I don't feel oppressed or I don't feel exploited in the way that you're saying," they say things like, "She's too blinded by her own oppression to see her experience for what it really is, and it really is the patriarchy." They find it necessary to interpret prostitutes' experience of their lives and then feed it back to the prostitutes to tell them what's really happening, whereas they wouldn't dare be so condescending or patronizing with any other group of women. Why is that?

But how can they hear us talk, how can they hear us when they can't even hear their own bodies? They are continually shaping it with their minds, whatever their bodies tell them, obviously, or they could never come up with this formula. Whatever their bodies are telling them somehow comes up through their minds, and then they shape what's comfortable. Where can they place that intellectually? They're shaping it and stopping it at the dam here. If they can't even hear themselves, how can they hear us? They're not even hearing their own bodies tell them, "Wait a minute, you know. I need to put this feeling that I have today somewhere. How can I integrate it in a positive way? I'm feeling a need to be assertive sexually." "Oh no, no, because I have to be on top." "I'm feeling like I need padding today." "Oh no, no, that's not politically correct." You suggest to a feminist, "Let's have some real fucking sleazy-type sex" or "Let's get down to fucking sweat, let's get down to some raunch," and she'll say, "Oh no, no, that's not right either. That's abuse." Or "That's a result of pornography." Feminists are so blocked sexually around what's politically correct, what's madonna-like.

LAURIE BELL: What is your response to some feminists' concern that some women are getting hurt in the sex trade?

CORP: That goes back to the question, "Can you be a police officer and not put your life in danger?" You don't even have to go that far. How about being a Becker's clerk on the night shift?

The judge in California said you can't rape the hooker, there's no such thing as raping a hooker. Then there's no such thing as holding up a store because they've laid their merchandise out for people to come in and get it. But we all know there's an understood agreement there. There are terms by which you can walk out with that merchandise. With prostitution, though, the judges say, "No, no. Those terms don't have to be respected." How can you be anyone walking down the street and not get hurt? I'll tell you how you can do it. It's real simple. You simply set up the support systems so the message is very clear to society: you can't do that. And you give them all the support.

I know Becker's people that have a switch that's right into the police station. How can that guy run a store and not get hurt? How can he lay his wares out to tempt people like that and not get hurt? And he does it in the dead of night! All alone at night in bad areas of town. And not to mention the cabbies. How can they not get hurt? We think we should close all those stores, get the cabs off the street. Stop the subways because, after all, there was a girl killed in the subway.

The whole thing about saving people from themselves is really offensive because it is patronizing. "We're putting these laws in there to protect you from yourself. You don't realize, dear, just how dangerous it can be out there.

"You don't realize how sick you are to put yourself in that

position. We know how sick you are, and we're going to prevent you from doing that because we know how much danger you're really in. And we're going to make sure you're going to stay in that kind of danger if you make that choice because we're going to make sure you can't go anywhere else. We're going to protect you from all of that; we're going to protect you from your choice. We're going to set up a situation where we create that danger so that we'll protect you from that danger, when you make that choice, by stopping you from making it."

Safety has never been a reason to stop people from doing things. We don't say to guys who want to drive a race car, "Oh no, dear, you can't do that. You might get hurt. It's very dangerous. There's an 80 percent chance that you'll die in a car crash." Now poor little men, they can't make that decision for themselves. You'd never use that explanation to stop guys from doing that. We only apply it to people who we feel aren't capable of making that decision for themselves. It's really patronizing. Of course they're capable of making that decision. Whores are an embarrassment to feminists because they're glaringly saying, "No, you're wrong. My experience and my life don't coalesce with yours."

Most violence takes place in long-term relationships, where people feel boxed in, where they can't make other choices, and those are the most violent home situations.

LAURIE BELL: What about the pimp?

CORP: Feminists have always tried to save us from the pimp. Ryan Hotchkiss lives with Val Scott. She takes money from Val when she's out of work. Technically speaking, she can be taken away for seven years. It's sort of the unwritten thing — we're not allowed to live with anyone, and we're not allowed to have a mate, and we're not allowed to give them any money.

You're not allowed to habitually be in the company of a prostitute. That makes you a pimp.

This means we're not allowed to have friends, we're not allowed to have lovers. These are the pimping laws that they're defending, which is a way of telling us that we can't have anybody. We're not good enough, and the only people that would be seen or caught dead around us are no-goods anyway because nobody decent would really associate with us. We're going to protect you from those no-goods. You ask a feminist, in Ryan's case, "Are you prepared to support these laws?" That's a graphic illustration, and we think it should be addressed. Feminists don't realize what they're saying to us. They're protecting their own lives because they're afraid their husbands will marry us. We don't want them anyway.

Imagine how threatened they must feel because some part of them knows that we're going to be pretty fucking good with their husbands. Imagine if it was okay to start mating with a whore. Can you imagine how threatened they would feel by that? If it was suddenly okay that the husband could actually take us home to momma? And men are just as bad. Do you know how many men are bad fucks? If women started to get the service and get a good fuck in them for a change, how many of them would leave their husbands?

These guys are terrified of that too. Because they don't even know where a woman's clit is, half these guys twenty years married. They don't even know how to find the hole. A lot of them say, "Well, I don't know if my wife has ever had an orgasm. I think she has. Well, I don't know if she really likes sex." Imagine if women suddenly had the sexual power and the wherewithal financially to be able to say, "I have the right to be satisfied and satiated sexually. And if he can't do it, then there's no disgrace about me getting on the phone and having someone come over, male or female." He doesn't want her to find out what a good cock is all about. Or a good pussy, for that matter.

As women get more financial power, more and more women are calling up escort services. There are now a couple of escort services in the Yellow Pages that advertise for women. It's the money, because they don't have the money. Not only that, they have not yet learned to give themselves permission to need that. They don't know how to say it's okay that they just have someone over for their own lustful purposes. They don't know how to do that yet.

The first step is getting a woman to understand that her sexual needs are what they are and they're valid. She's entitled to that. She doesn't know how to say okay to that. It's okay if she goes to a bar and talks to a guy for a while, and they sort of fall in. "Well, it just sort of happened that way." But she doesn't know how to say, "I need to be sexually serviced. I know exactly what I need. I need someone to do this and this to me, and I don't want to have to explain, and I don't want to do something back. I want to just lie there and be satiated, and I will pay this to do it. I'll compromise this amount." Now doesn't that sound ideal to you?

LAYERS

Written and Performed by

Shawna Dempsey

Shawna comes on stage dressed only in plastic wrap, which she has wrapped around her body.

I'M BOUND AND TIED. Now some of you might assume I'm portraying a pornography model in an S/M situation. Or a kinky housewife waiting for her hubby to get home. Wrong. I'm just being myself; your average feminist at your average Politics of Pornography conference. In fact, I'm wearing my traditional feminist costume: layers and layers and layers and layers of theory and criticism.

Now there's nothing wrong with theory and criticism, but there's so much of them, and they all conflict with each other! It simply leaves me tied in knots. Especially on the issue of pornography:

"We should always veer to the left to avoid being co-opted by the right-wing pro-censorship movement." Or "Pornography perpetrates violence against women and should be stopped at all costs, no matter who else is on the bandwagon."

How about these? "The sex trade worker is a victim." Or "The sex trade worker uses her sexual power to exploit men." Or "The sex trade worker is our sister." Or "She's not my sister."

It makes a discussion difficult, doesn't it? I mean, it's hard to know what to say. And it seems you can't talk about porn without talking about erotica: "Erotica's good. Pornography's bad." Or "If people had the real thing, they wouldn't need images." Or "Lesbian porn is different."

Finally, there's something we feminists hear more than anything: "You don't know what you're talking about! You don't work in the industry."

So in light of all this, I've decided not to perform for you. I'm really sorry, but I would invariably offend you all if I were to perform a piece about pornography. Now this isn't anyone's fault. It's simply too sensitive an issue right now.

And I am too good a feminist to knowingly offend a sister.

AFTERWORD

MUCH HAS HAPPENED IN Canada regarding pornography and prostitution since November 1985. Most of the activity has been inspired by the recent federal legislation on prostitution, Bill C-49, now Section 195.1 of the Criminal Code, and that on pornography, Bill C-54. The response to these two bills has been widespread.

Bill C-49 has been used extensively throughout Canada to arrest prostitutes, primarily those working on the street. Many of those charged have pleaded guilty and been fined. Others have contested the charge and had it struck down. The constitutionality of Section 195.1 has been challenged before courts of appeal in British Columbia, Ontario, and Nova Scotia.

The Canadian Organization for the Rights of Prostitutes has become a member of the National Action Committee on the Status of Women. At NAC's 1986 annual meeting CORP introduced an emergency resolution calling for the repeal of C-49, opposition to "any and all legislation which seeks to limit the personal and business lives of adult prostitutes," and support for the agenda of prostitutes to work for "empowerment in their working agenda." This resolution carried, but with a great deal of division and differing points of view. As a result, a Prostitution Committee was struck.

At the 1987 annual meeting of NAC the Prostitution Committee brought forward more resolutions, including the repeal of the section of the Criminal Code dealing with "living on the avails" and opposition to the forced testing and/or quarantining of prostitutes for AIDS and other sexually transmitted diseases. Most members agreed that there was definitely no unanimity in

NAC concerning the right of prostitutes to work and the dignity of that work.

The Association for the Safety of Prostitutes, now named POWER, has been active especially in Vancouver. Marie Arrington, a spokesperson, has been publicly addressing the implications of Bill C-49 for the safety of prostitutes generally and in particular the murder of five Vancouver prostitutes in a two-year period.

A national group called Citizens Organization to Repeal Prostitution-Related Laws (CORPRL) was established early in 1987. It calls for the decriminalization of prostitution and affirms the dignity and worth of prostitutes and their work.

In Toronto a board of directors was formed in 1986 to begin a self-help project for prostitutes called Maggies. The project plans to include a storefront, self-defence training, child care, and legal information by and for prostitutes.

There has been outspoken opposition to the proposed Bill C-54, which will censor sex-related material. Writers, artists, gay men, lesbians, and feminists have been in the forefront of this battle. In response to the introduction of the legislation, the Canadian Committee Against Customs Censorship was formed in Toronto, and the Coalition for the Right to View was formed in Vancouver. Public protests and press conferences have been organized, and further activities are planned.

There are three areas that demand the attention of feminists. First, within the feminist movement we need to continue our dialogue about analyses of and strategies toward pornography and prostitution. We need to address the conflict between an anti-pornography and an anti-censorship view, between a stance that supports sex trade workers and one that regards them as victims.

Second, we need to move beyond the identified feminist community and initiate and maintain a relationship with the women working in the sex trade. Whatever our point of view, we must be informed by sex trade workers themselves.

Lastly, we need to take public action. We are compelled to respond to legislative changes and the results of their implementation. The well-being of the feminist movement and the lives of many women depend on our conscientious attention to these tasks.

BIOGRAPHICAL NOTES

MARIE ARRINGTON is a founding member of the Alliance for the Safety of Prostitutes, now known as POWER, in Vancouver, British Columbia. She is an active proponent of decriminalizing prostitution and is an organizer in Vancouver.

LAURIE BELL is a community activist doing advocacy work for people with disabilities. She helped organize the conference Challenging Our Images: The Politics of Pornography and Prostitution, and serves on the Board of Directors of Maggies, a self-help project for street prostitutes. Also a sometime songwriter and member of the Fly By Night Dyke Band, Bell works on the March 8 Coalition planning International Women's Day.

CHRISTINE BOYLE is a feminist legal theorist who teaches law at Dalhousie Law School, Halifax, Nova Scotia.

VARDA BURSTYN is a writer and teacher as well as activist in the anti-censorship movement. She is the editor of *Women Against Censorship*, published in 1985 by Douglas & McIntyre, Vancouver.

CATHY is a prostitute who operates an escort service in Toronto.

SUSAN G. COLE has written and spoken extensively about pornography and has been active in the battle against violence against women. She is a journalist and a member of the *Broadside* editorial collective in Toronto, Ontario.

AMBER COOKE is a retired veteran stripper. She has worked as a life skills coach for strippers and conducted an extensive study for the Elizabeth Fry Society of the service needs of street prostitutes in Toronto.

CORP (The Canadian Organization for the Rights of Prostitutes) works to decriminalize prostitution and support prostitutes who are arrested or harmed for doing their work.

SHAWNA DEMPSEY is an actress. She is a member of the Company of Sirens, a feminist theatre company in Toronto.

MARY JOHNSON is a veteran stripper. She is a past president of the Canadian Association of Burlesque Entertainers (CABE).

LESBIANS OF COLOUR is a group doing anti-racist education in Toronto. It has participated in many organizing efforts, including the March 8th Coalition.

JOAN NESTLE is a writer, teacher, and founding member of the Lesbian Herstory Archives in New York City. She is the author of the forthcoming book, *A Restricted Country*, to be published by Firebrand Books, Ithaca.

SHEILAH NOONAN is a feminist legal theorist who is currently at the Institute of Criminology Cambridge University.

MARTHA O'CAMPO is a member of the Committee to Advance the Movement for Democracy and Independence — Philippines (CAMDI—Philippines), formerly the Committee Against the Marcos Dictatorship — Philippine Solidarity Network—Toronto Chapter (CAMD—PSN).

ONTARIO PUBLIC INTEREST RESEARCH GROUP (OPIRG) — TORONTO is an organization promoting public interest research, especially among graduate students at the University of Toronto. OPIRG sponsors many projects, both written and active, on a variety of environmental, social, and political concerns.

PETAL ROSE is a striptease artist and prostitute who has worked in Toronto the Good for eighteen years.

VALERIE SCOTT is a Toronto prostitute. She is a spokesperson for the Canadian Organization for the Rights of Prostitutes (CORP).

MARGO ST. JAMES hails from San Francisco, California. She represents the sex trade workers' rights organization COYOTE (Call Off Your Old Tired Ethics). For ten years she has been actively promoting dialogue between sex trade workers and other members of the community.

MARIANA VALVERDE is a writer and activist in Toronto. She teaches women's studies at the University of Toronto and is the author of *Sex, Power and Pleasure*, published in 1986 by Women's Press, Toronto.

GLOSSARY

With thanks to Susan G. Cole and Gary Kinsman

BILL C-49: A proposed new federal law on prostitution that passed its third and final reading in the House of Commons the week prior to the conference. It is now Section 195.1 of the Criminal Code and reads:

(1) Every person who in a public place or in any place open to public view
   (a) stops or attempts to stop any motor vehicle,
   (b) impedes the free flow of pedestrian or vehicular traffic or ingress to or egress from the premises adjacent to that place, or
   (c) stops or attempts to stop any person or in any manner communicates or attempts to communicate with any person for the purpose of engaging in prostitution or of obtaining the sexual services of a prostitute is guilty of an offence punishable on summary conviction.

(2) In this section, "public place" includes any place to which the public have access as of right or by invitation, express or implied, and any motor vehicle located in a public place or in any place open to public view 1985, c. 50, s.1.

BILL C-114: Legislation censoring pornography introduced by Justice Minister John Crosbie in June 1986. It was revamped and reintroduced by the current Minister of Justice, Ray Hnatyshyn, as Bill C-54 on May 4, 1987. The bill defines six categories of pornography that would be illegal to produce, import, or sell in

Canada. Contained within these categories are depictions of "attempting to cause or appearing to cause ... impairment of the body" and "sexually violent conduct" as well as "masturbation," "ejaculation," and "vaginal, anal or oral intercourse." In addition, sexually explicit material cannot be sold to anyone under the age of eighteen, and the depiction of anyone under the age of eighteen or who "appears to be" under the age of eighteen would be criminalized.

PROCURING LAWS: Contained within Section 195 of the Canadian Criminal Code, which reads:

(1) Everyone who
   (a) procures, attempts to procure or solicits a person to have illicit sexual intercourse with another person, whether in or out of Canada,
   (b) inveigles or entices a person who is not a prostitute or a person of known immoral character to a common bawdy-house or house of assignation for the purpose of illicit sexual intercourse or prostitution,
   (c) knowingly conceals a person in a common bawdy-house or house of assignation,
   (d) procures or attempts to procure a person to become, whether in or out of Canada, a prostitute,
   (e) procures or attempts to procure a person to leave the usual place of abode of that person in Canada, if that place is not a common bawdy-house, with intent that the person may become an inmate or frequenter of a common bawdy-house, whether in or out of Canada,
   (f) on the arrival of a person in Canada, directs or causes the person to be directed or takes or causes that person to be taken to a common bawdy-house or house of assignation,
   (g) procures a person to enter or leave Canada, for the purpose of prostitution,

(h)   for the purposes of gain, exercises control, direction or influence over the movements of a person in such manner as to show that he is aiding, abetting or compelling that person to engage in or carry on prostitution with any or generally,

(i)   applies or administers to a person or causes that person to take any drug, intoxicating liquor, matter or thing with the intent to stupefy or overpower that person in order thereby to enable any person to have illicit sexual intercourse with that person, or

(j)   lives wholly or in part on the avails of prostitution of another person, is guilty of an indictable offence and is liable to imprisonment for ten years.

(2)   Evidence that a person lives with or is habitually in the company of prostitutes, or lives in a common bawdy-house or house of assignation is, in the absence of evidence to the contrary, proof that the person lives on the avails of prostitution.

BADGELY REPORT: A Canadian government report entitled the *Badgely Committee Report on Sexual Offences Against Children and Youth*, published by the Department of Supply and Services, Ottawa, 1984.

JOHN CROSBIE: Member of Parliament for the Progressive Conservative party. He served as justice minister and was responsible for introducing Bill C-49.

ANDREA DWORKIN: A key activist in the anti-pornography movement and the author of *Pornography: Men Possessing Women*, *Ice and Fire*, and *Intercourse*.

FRASER REPORT: A Canadian government report entitled the *Fraser Committee Report on Pornography and Prostitution*, published by the

Department of Supply and Services, Ottawa, 1985. Aspects of this report provided the foundation for the current Canadian legislation on pornography and prostitution.

CATHARINE MACKINNON: An anti-pornography feminist and legal scholar. Her views on pornography and its meaning are contained in *Feminism Unmodified*, published in 1987 by Harvard University Press.

MINNEAPOLIS ORDINANCE: A proposed legal approach to pornography co-authored by Catharine MacKinnon and Andrea Dworkin. The ordinance, and model ordinances that followed, defines pornography as a practice of sex discrimination. It would entitle women to take legal action against producers and consumers of pornography by making four activities legally actionable:

1. Coercion into pornography.
2. Having porn forced on you.
3. Assault caused by pornography.
4. Trafficking in pornography.

The ordinance was passed by the Minneapolis City Council but repeatedly vetoed by the mayor. A version was passed, but in a series of court cases all the way up to the Supreme Court it was found to be unconstitutional.

NAC: The National Action Committee on the Status of Women, a Canadian national coalition of women's groups.

Printed in Canada